This book is dedicated to
all the people who are sick of
coloring gardens, dolphins,
goddamn mandalas,
and doodle art. ;)

A NEBULOUS COLORING BOOK

FILL IN THE BLOT

A NEBULOUS COLORING BOOK

IKE-EWE
a division of
KEZIA CARTER STUDIO
2017
KEZIACARTERSTUDIO.COM

TEST PAGE

SUGGESTED MATERIALS

colored pencils, pens/gel pens, crayons, whatever you want...

We've had one, yes. But what about a
SECOND TEST PAGE?

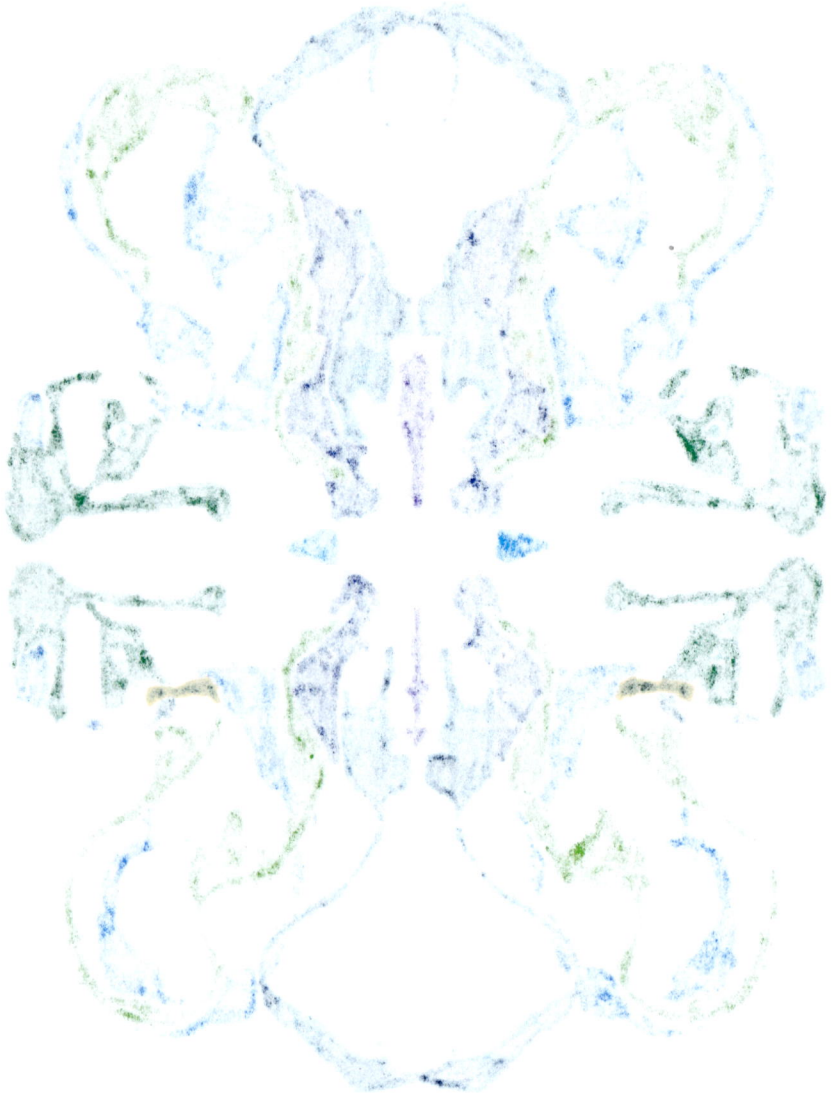

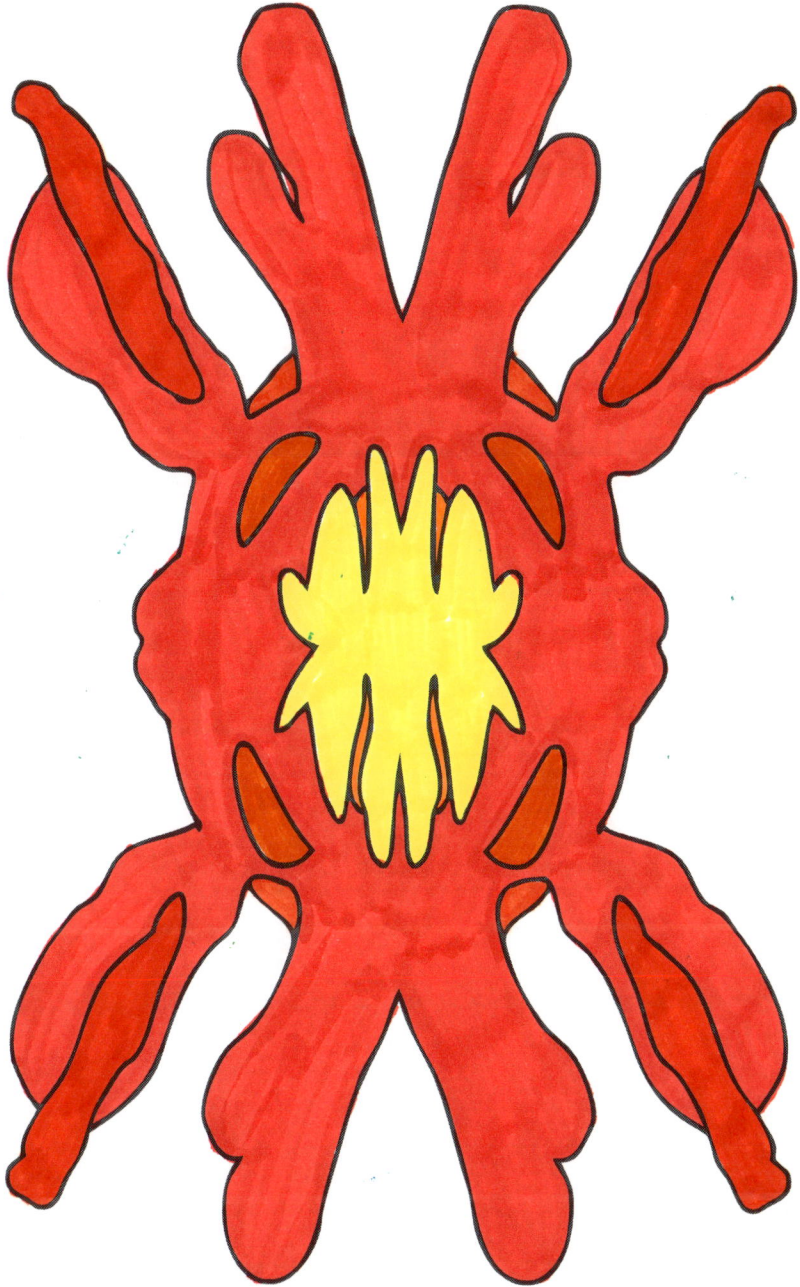

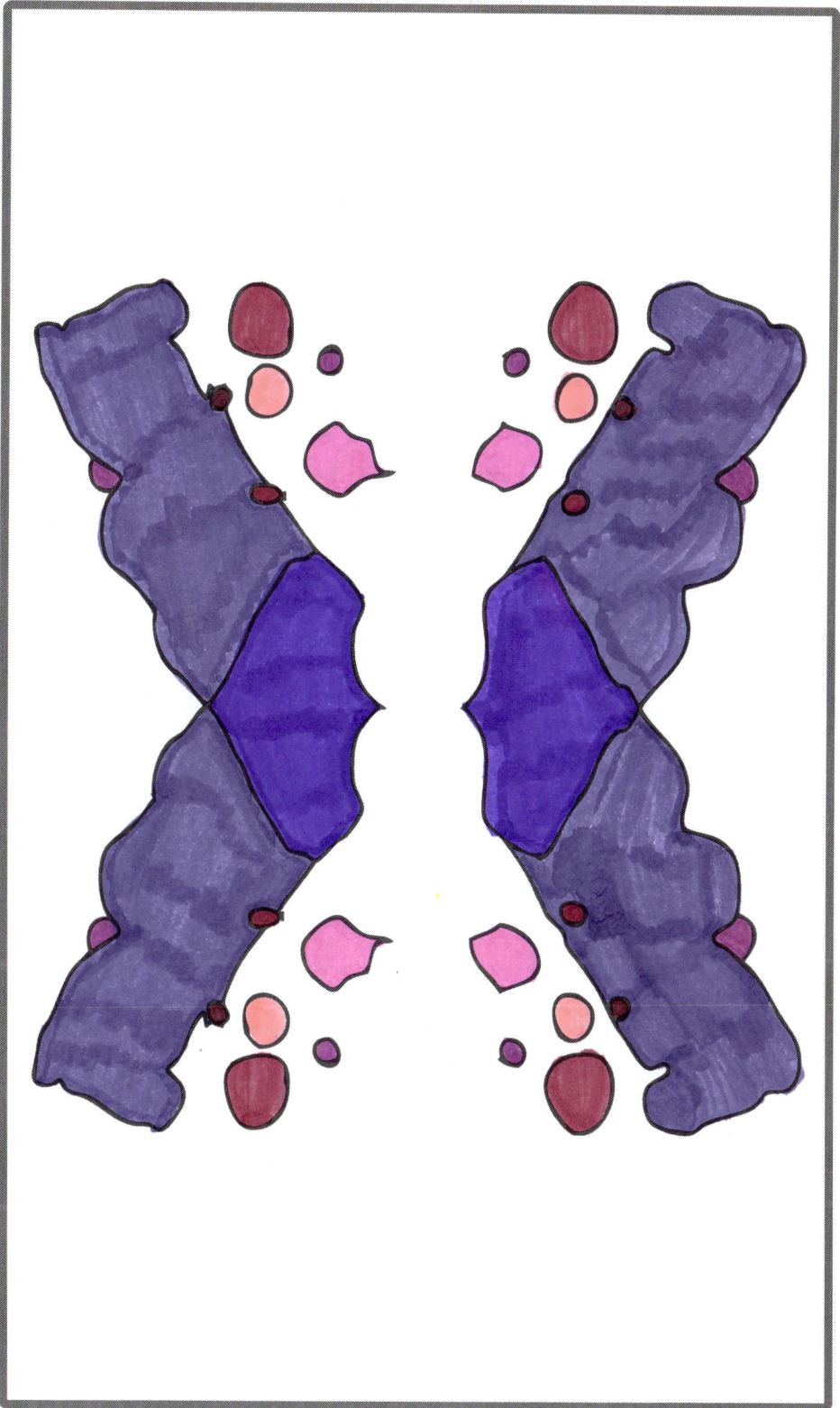

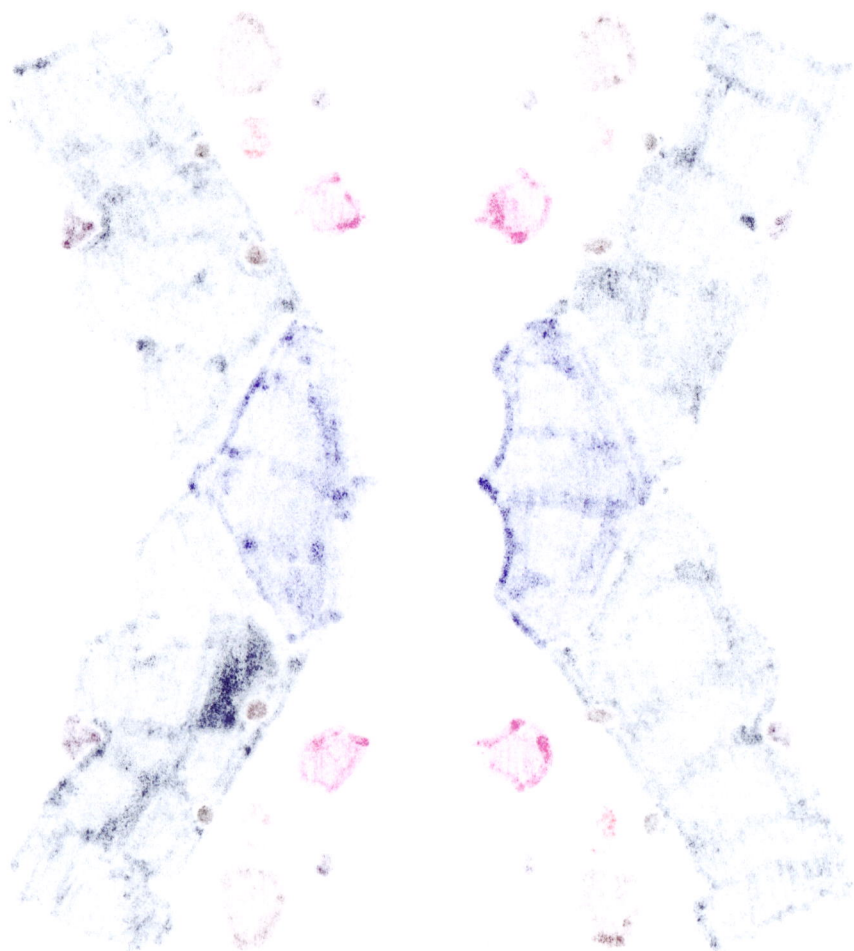

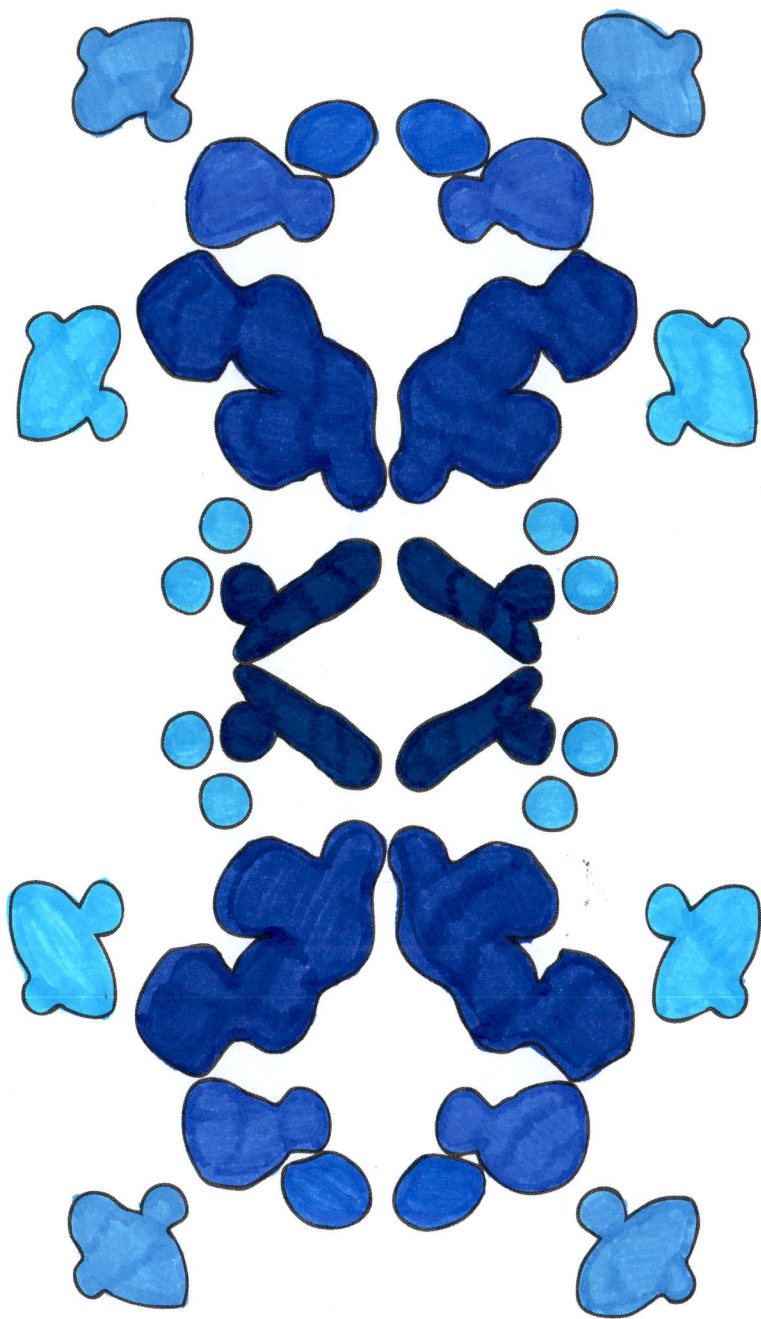

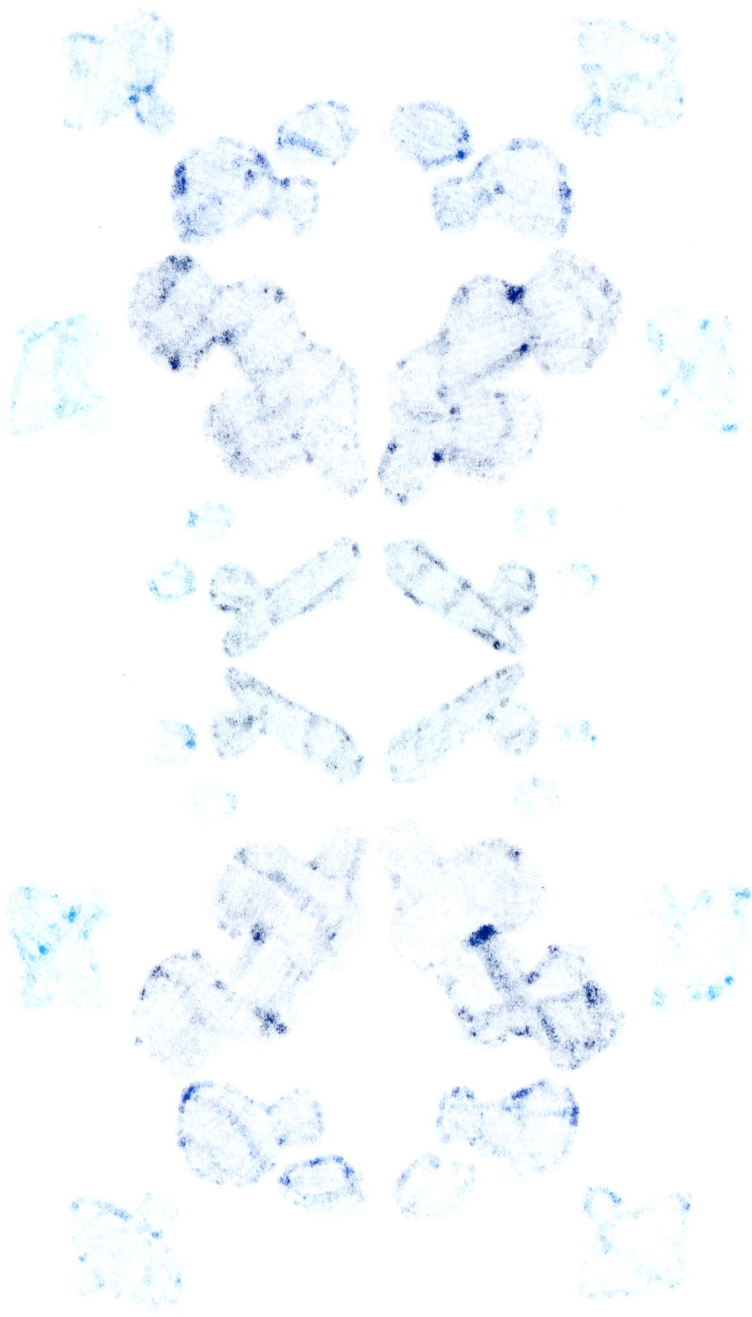

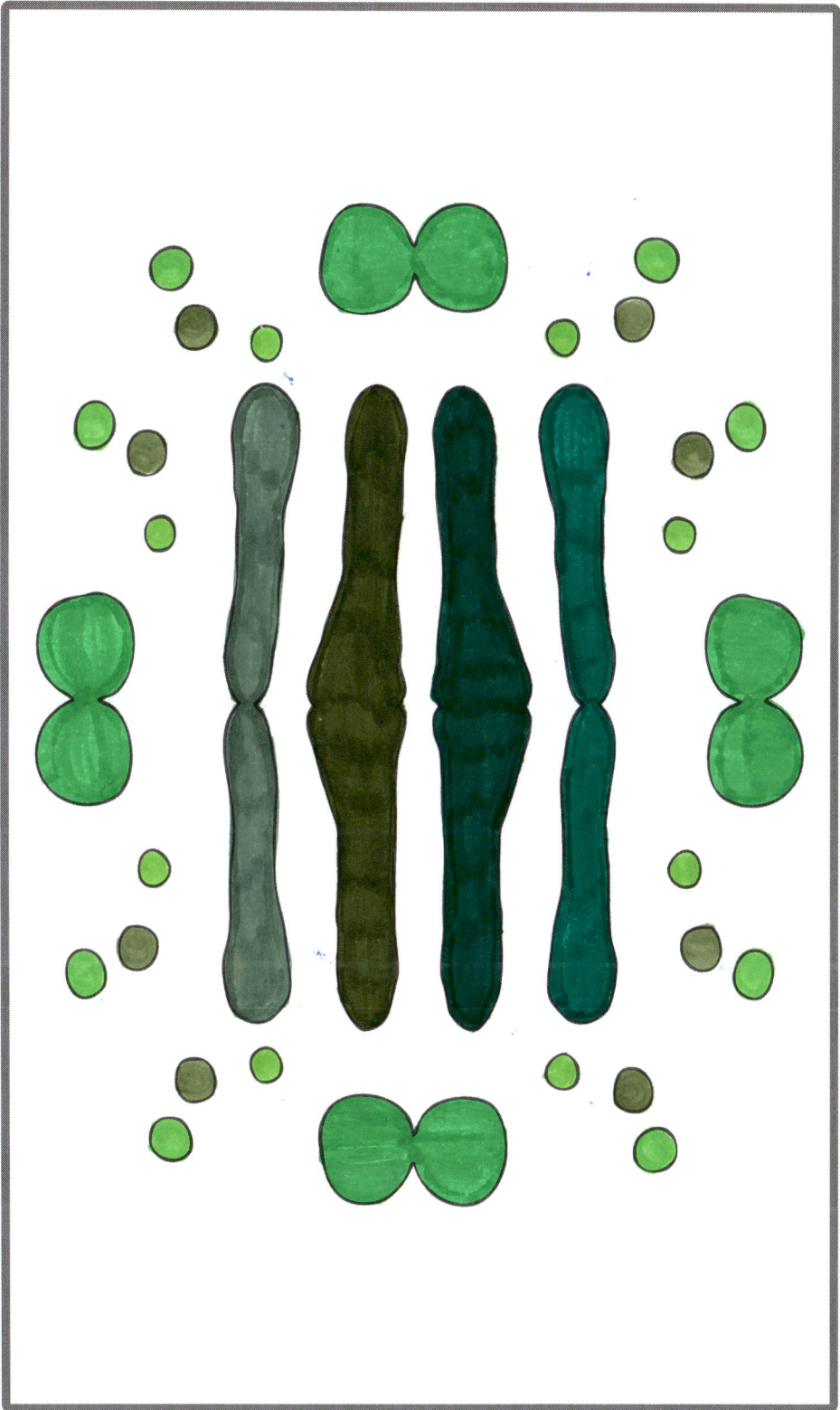

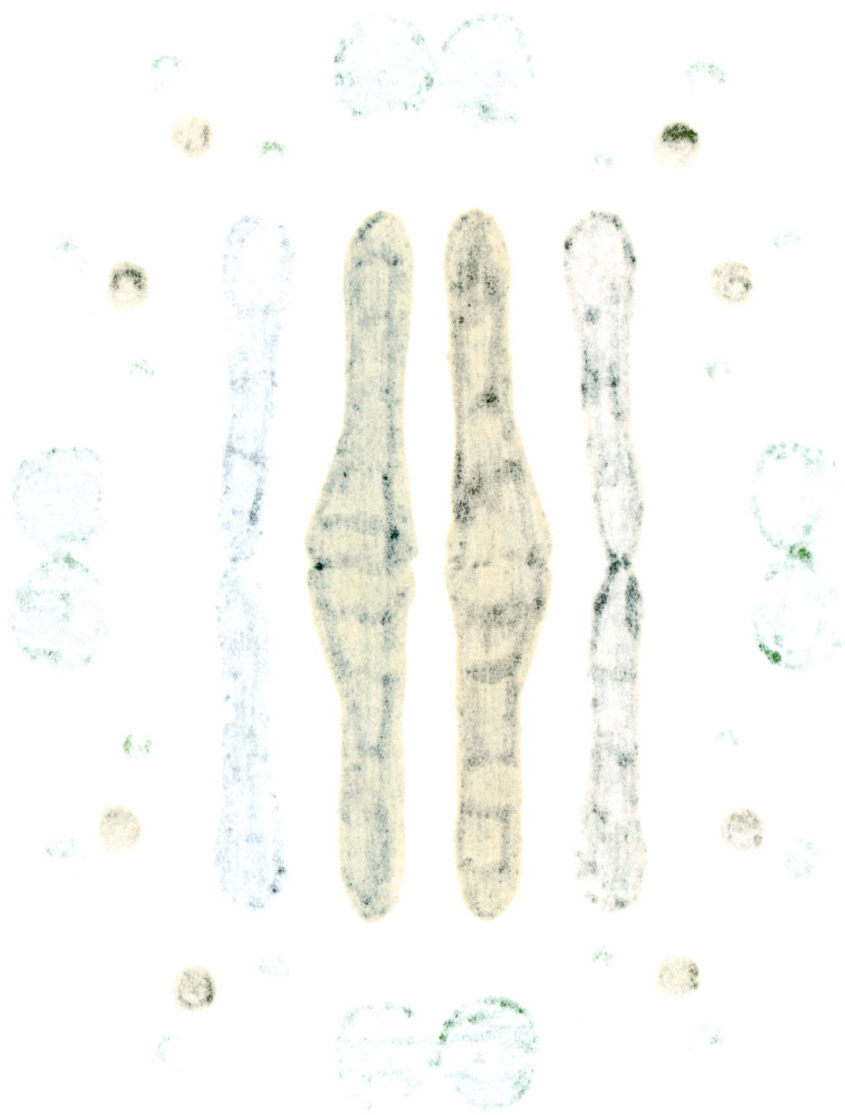

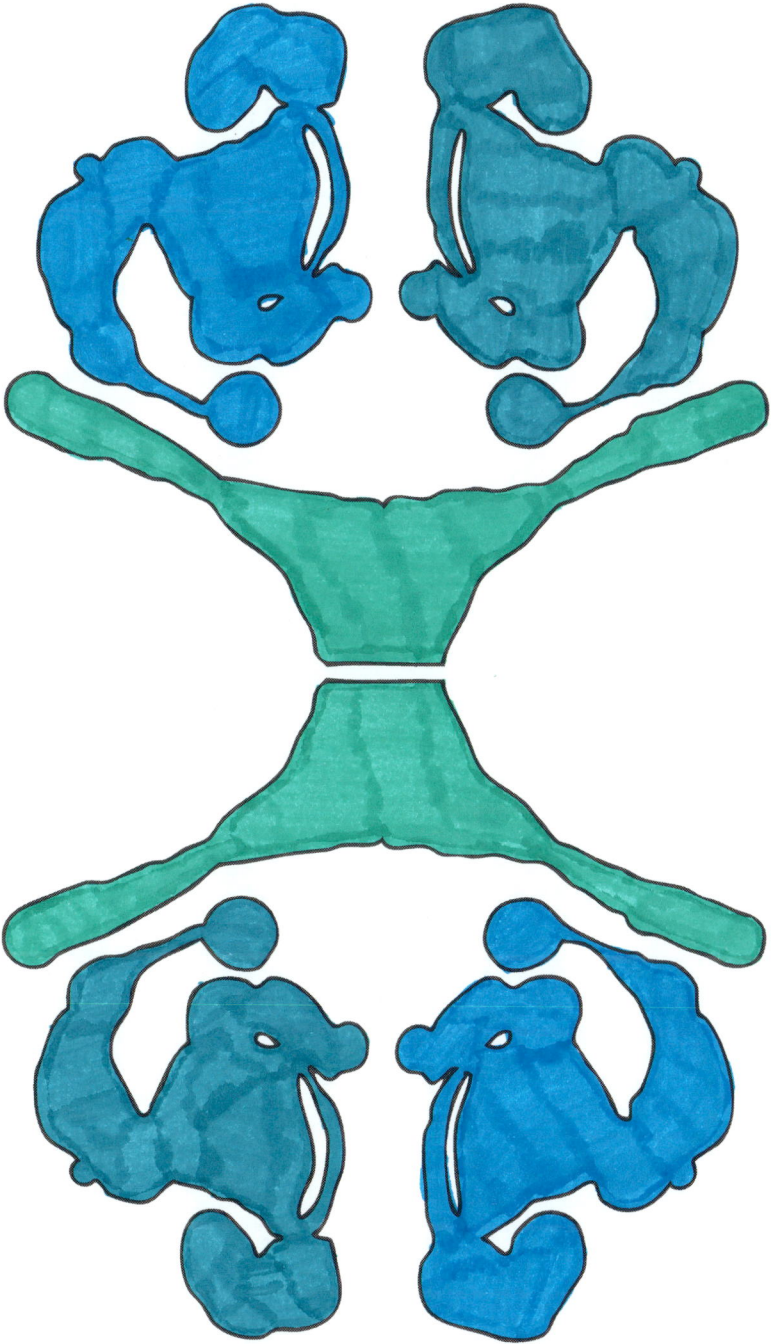

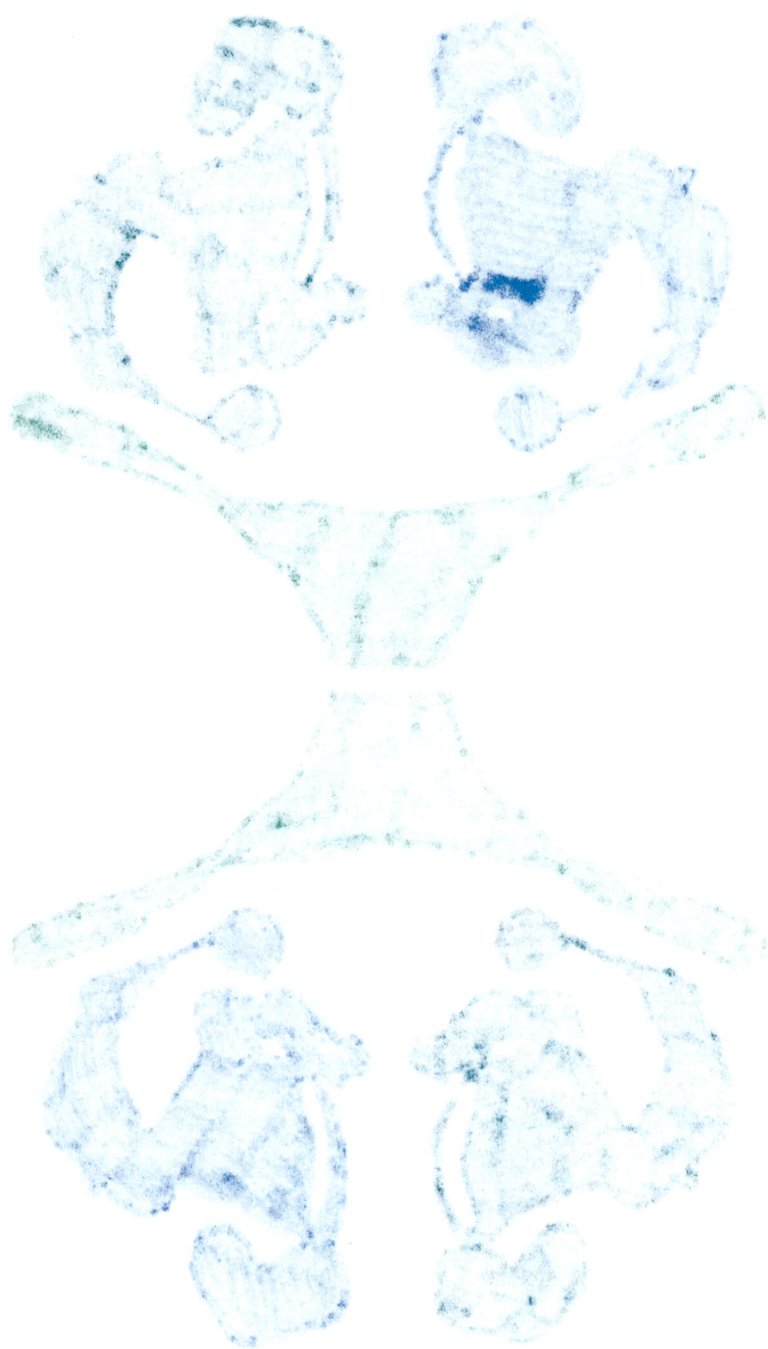

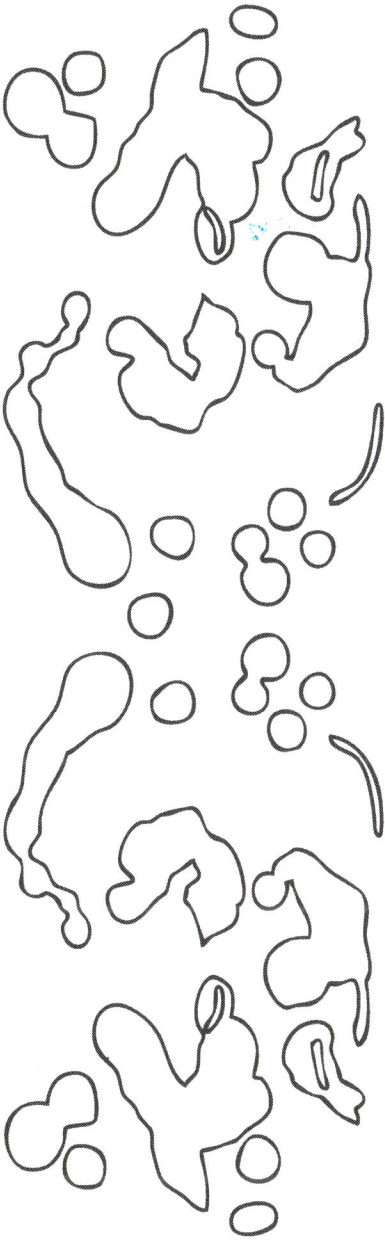

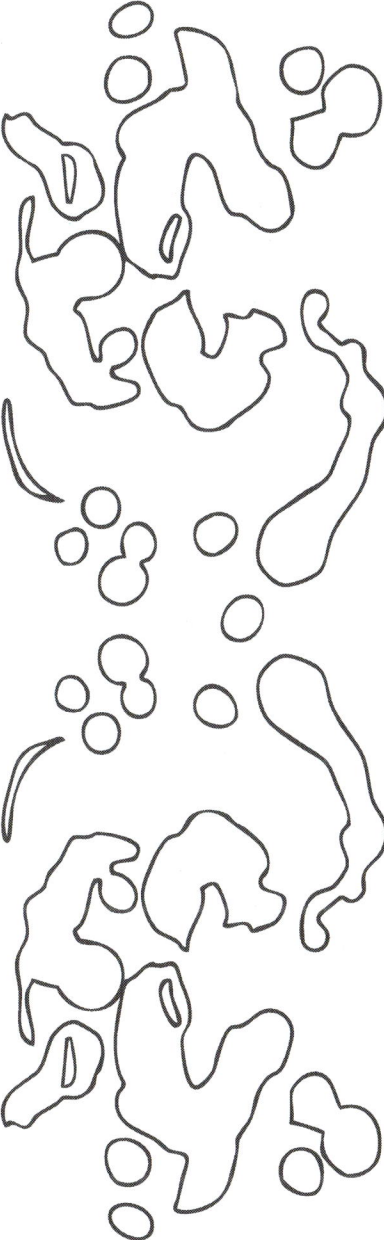

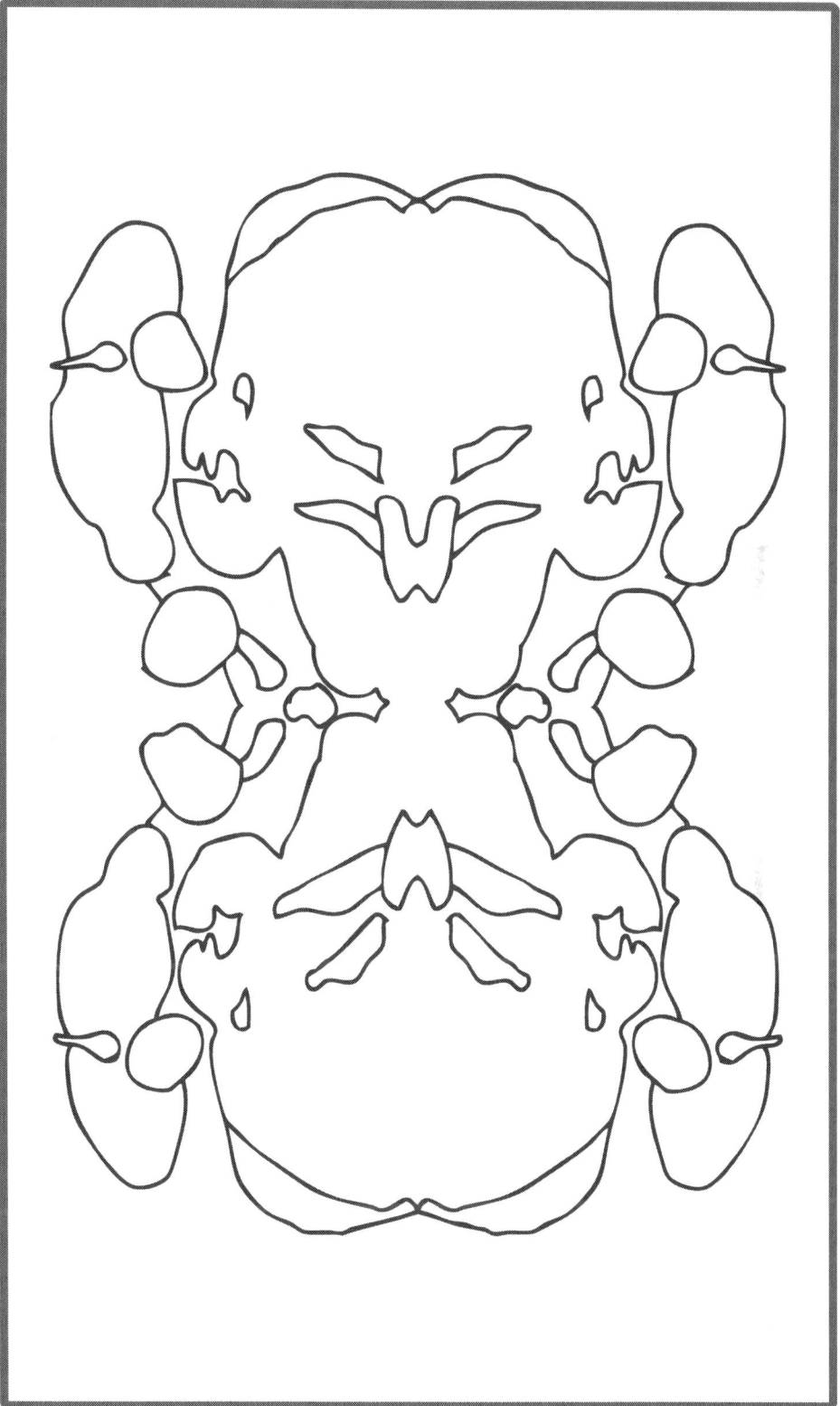

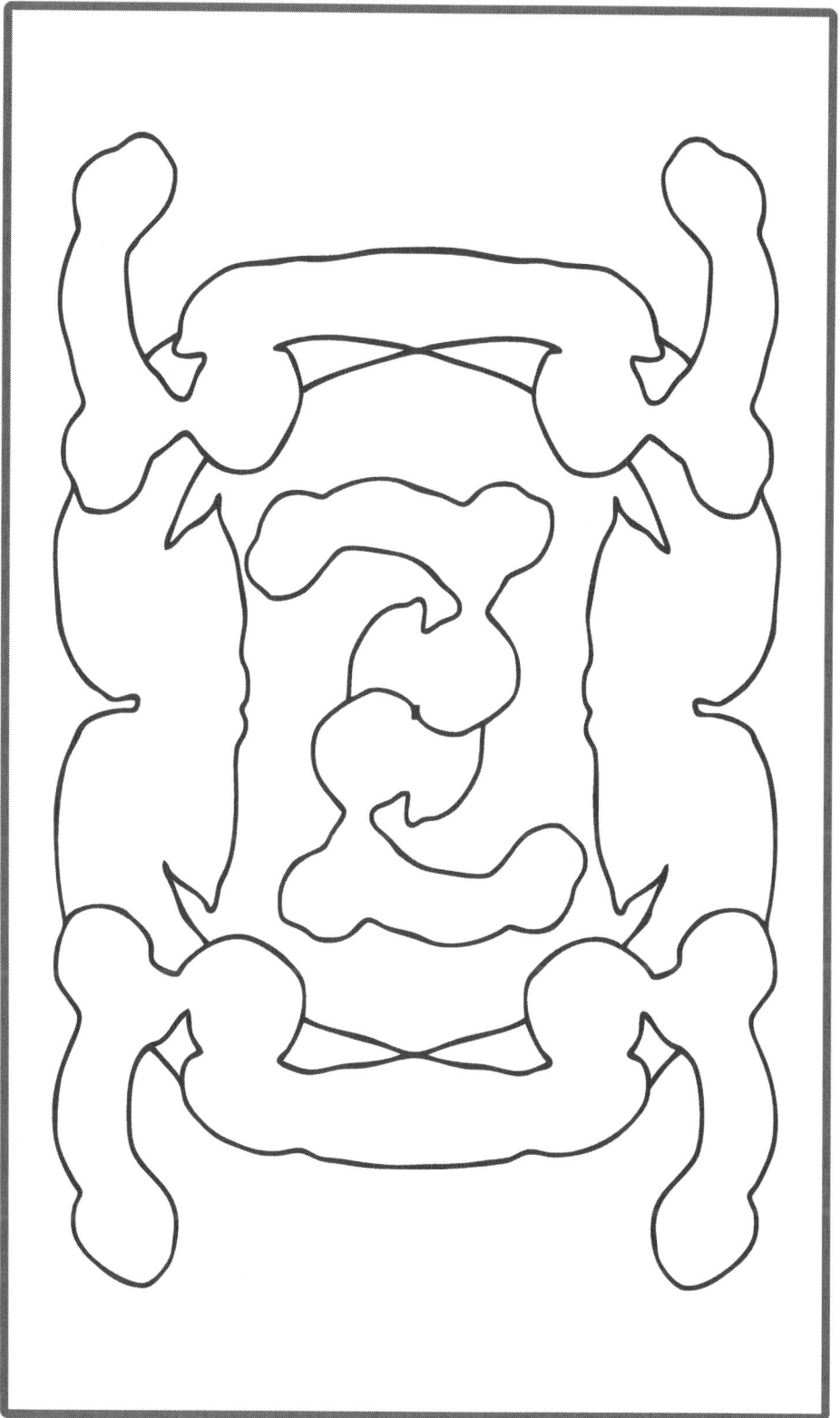

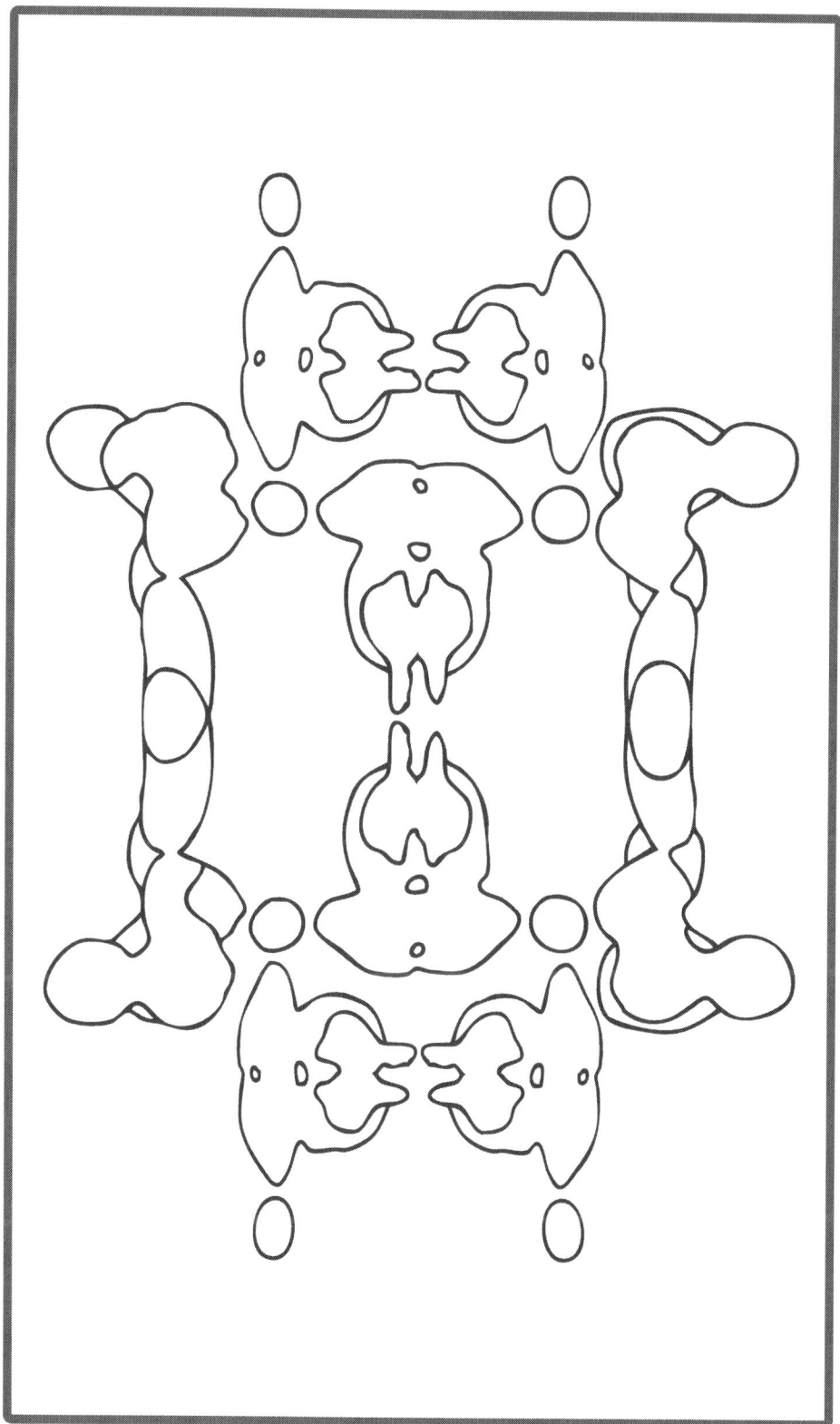

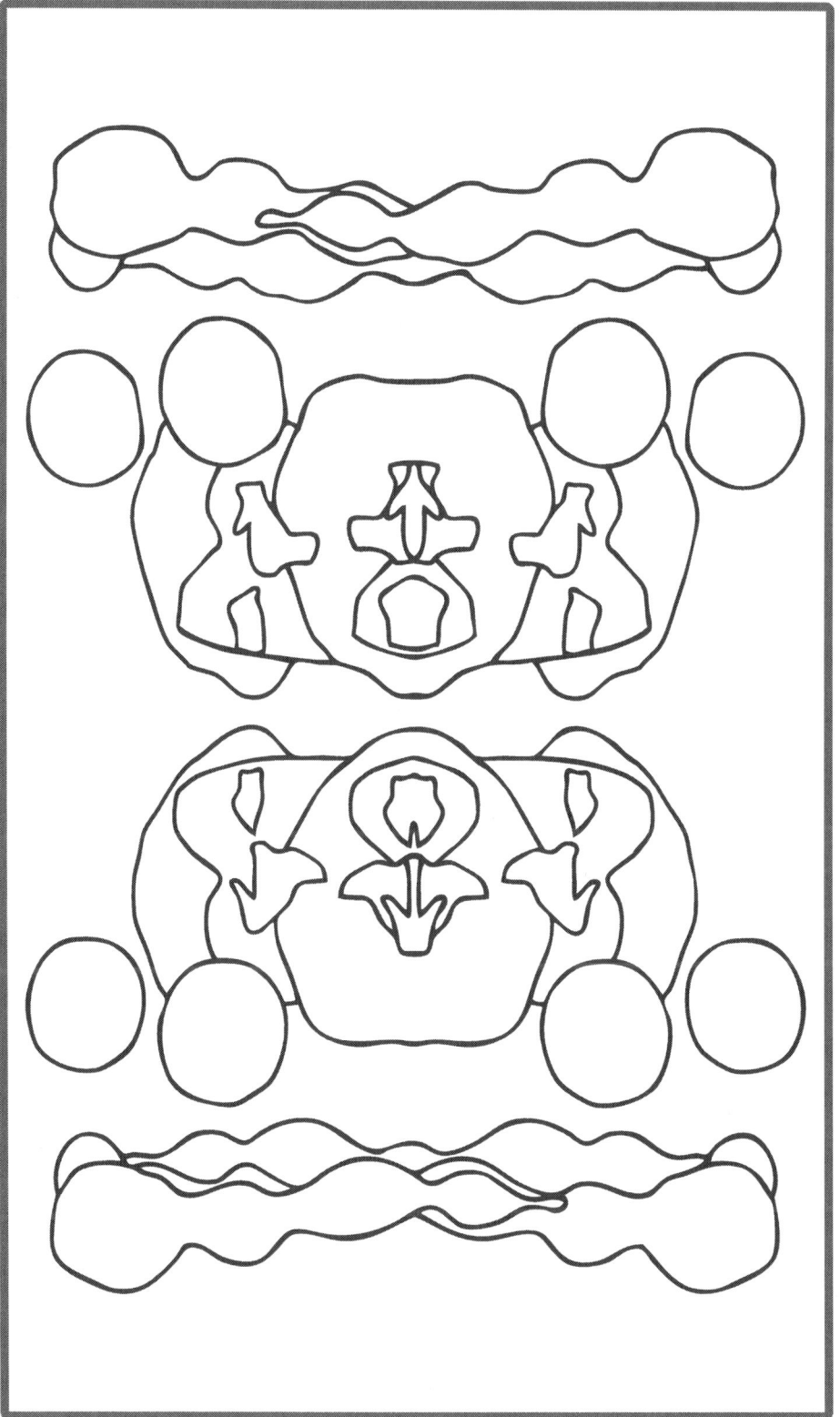

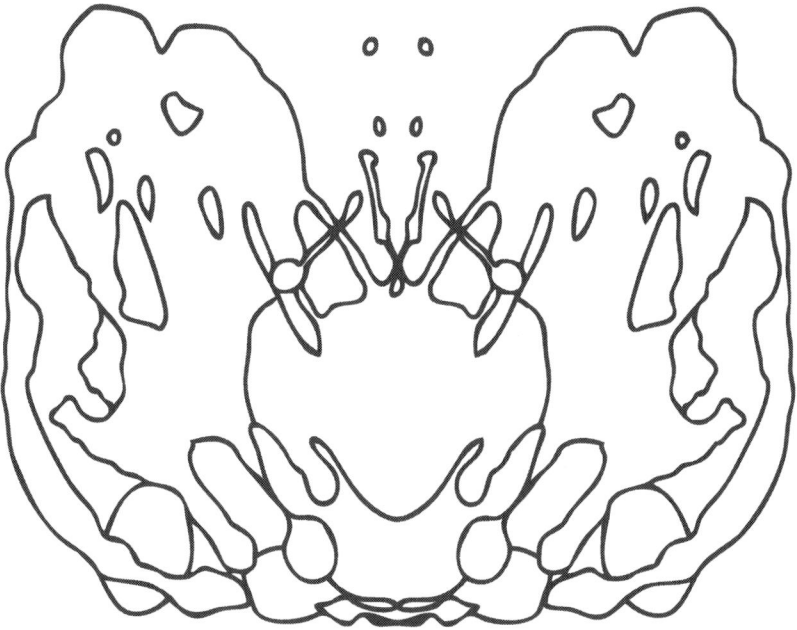

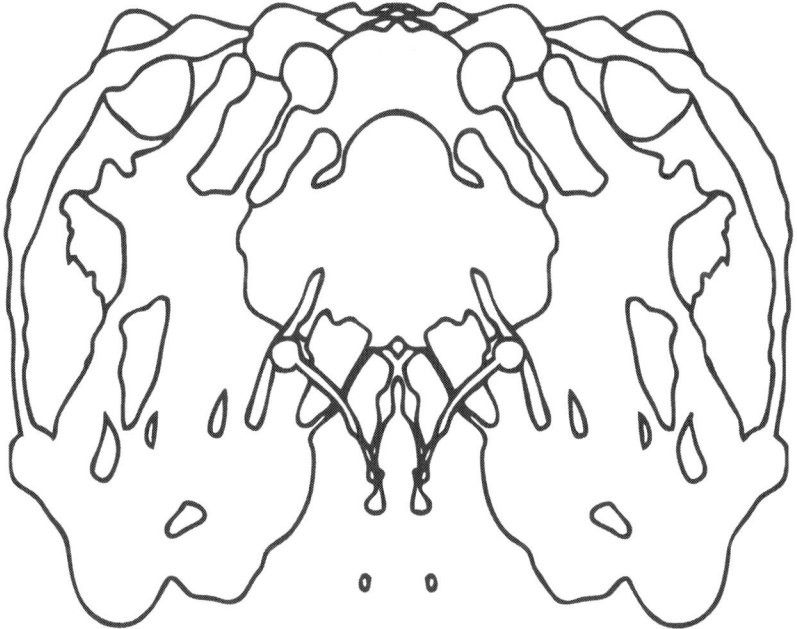

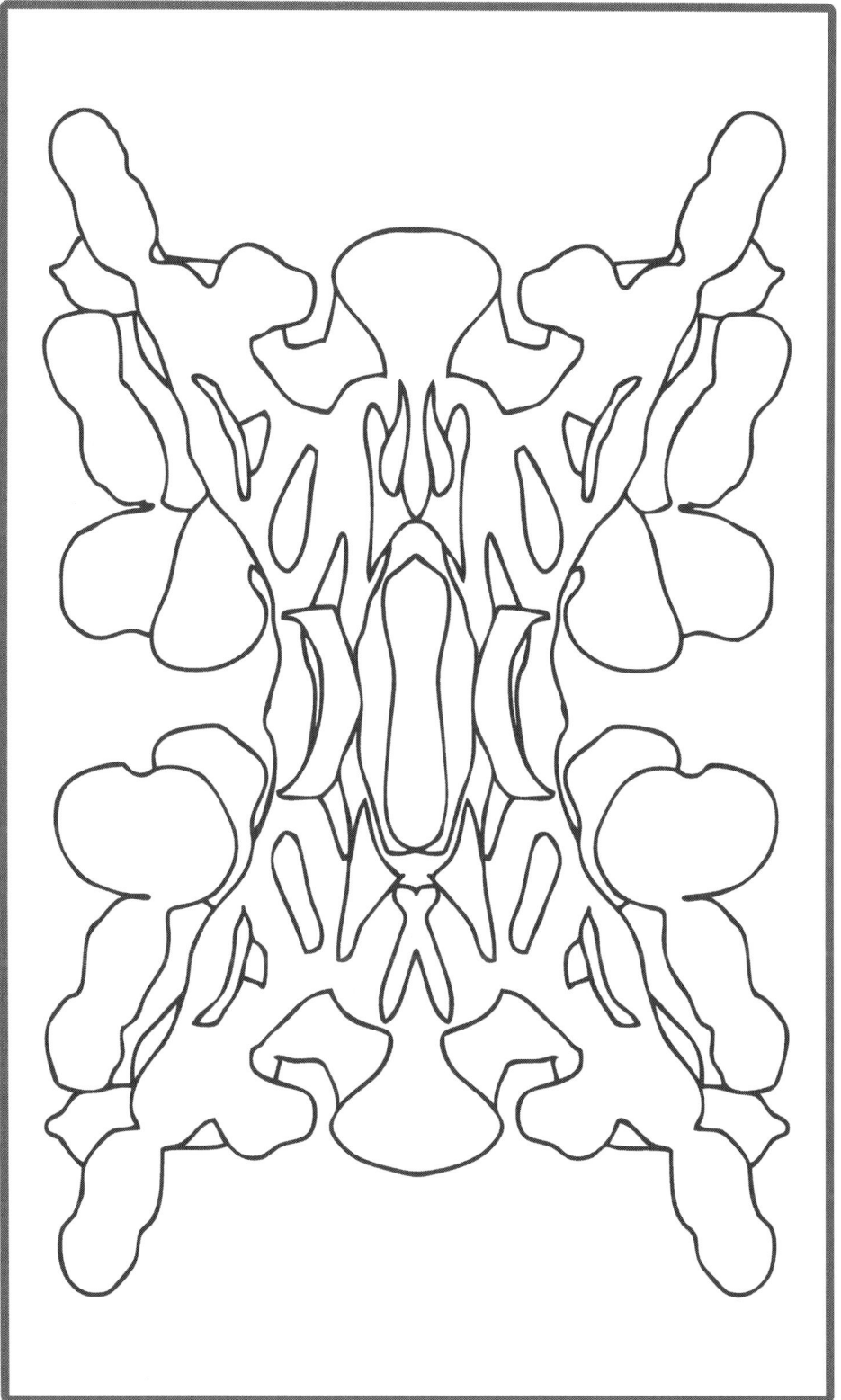

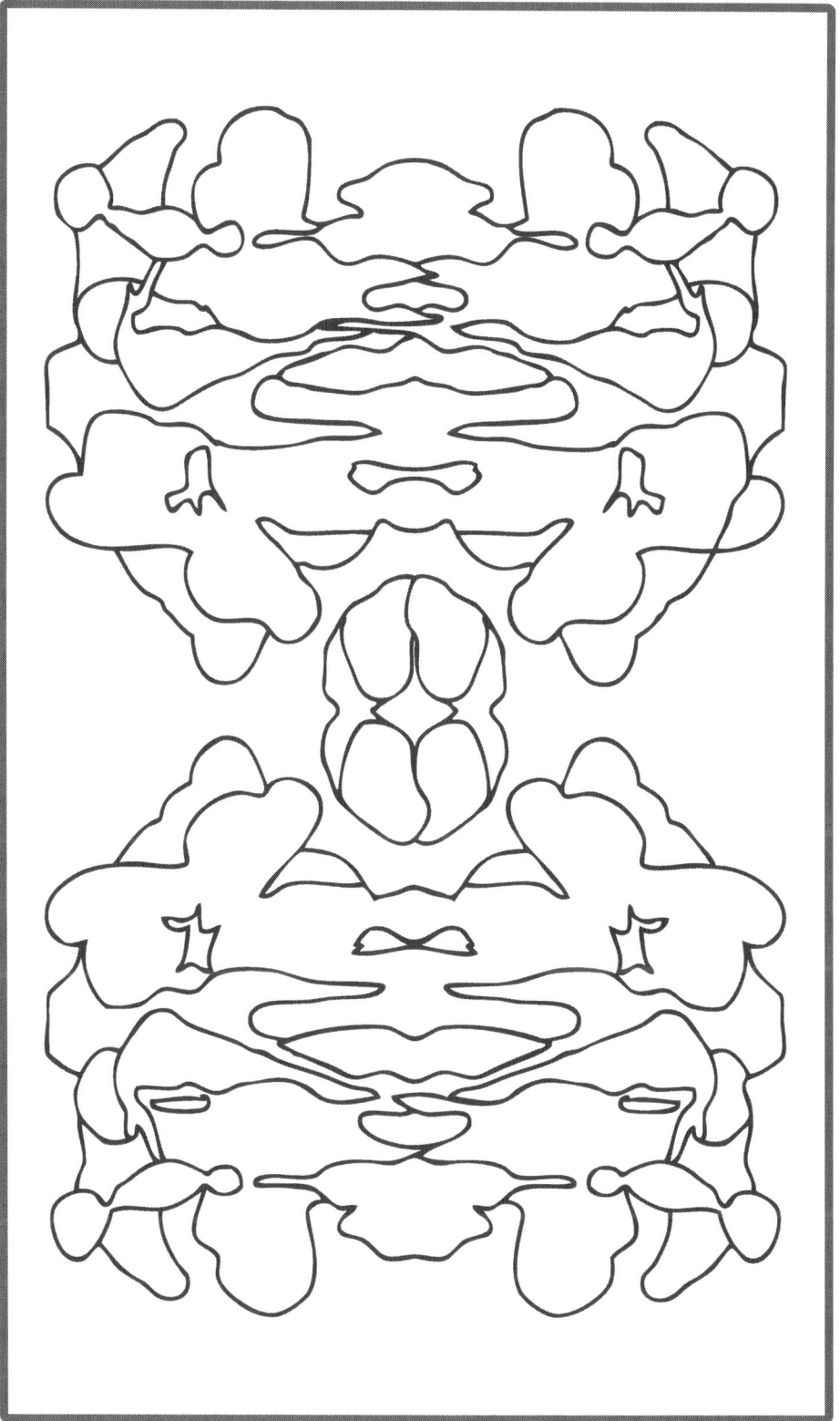

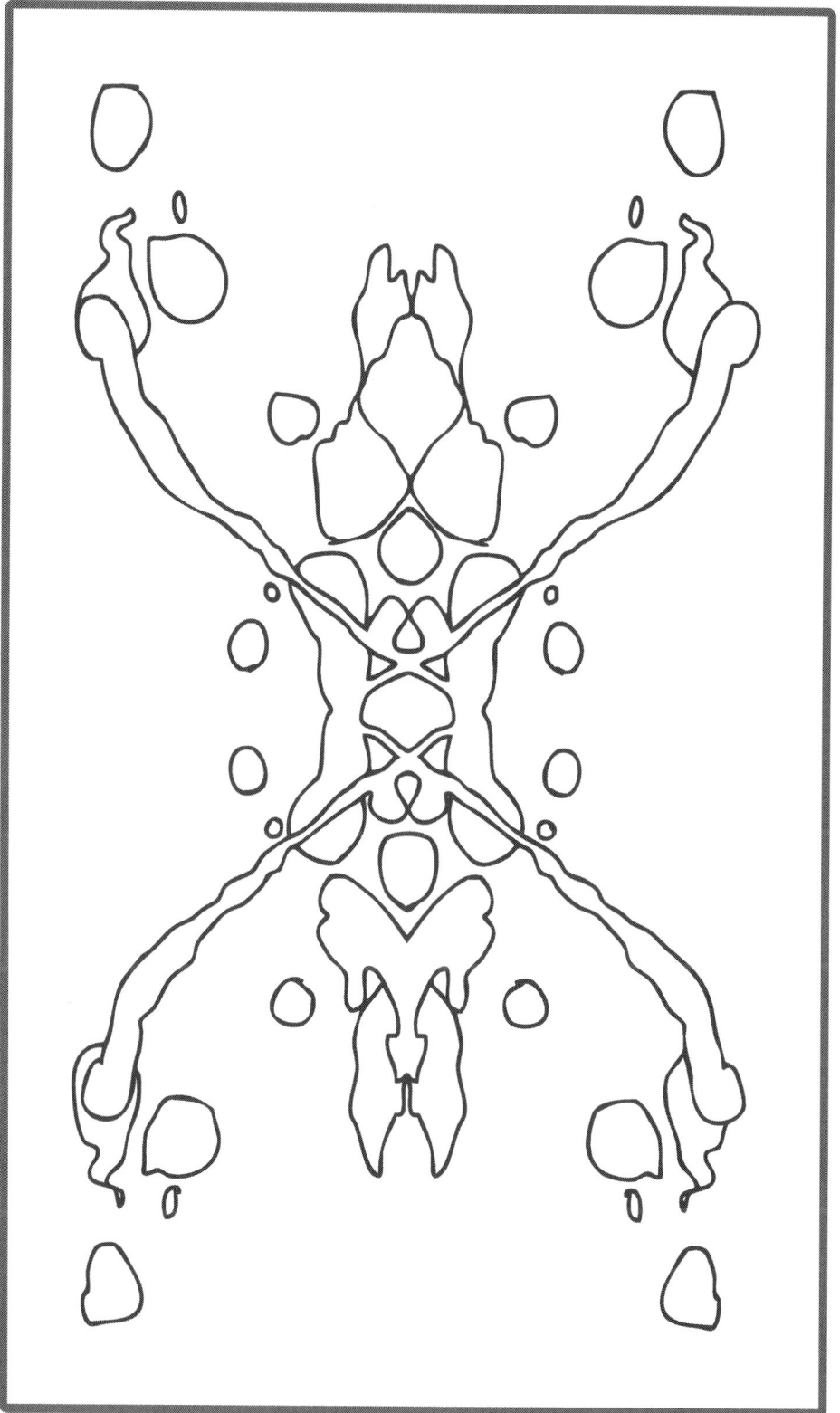

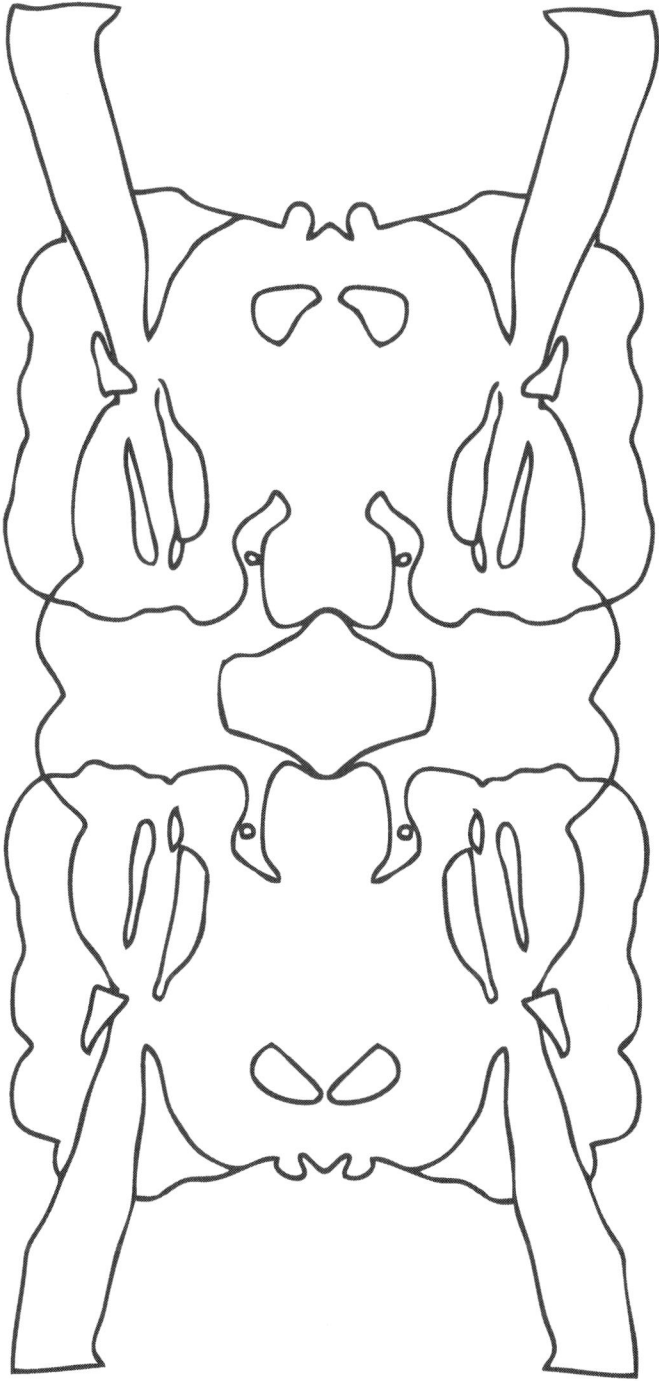

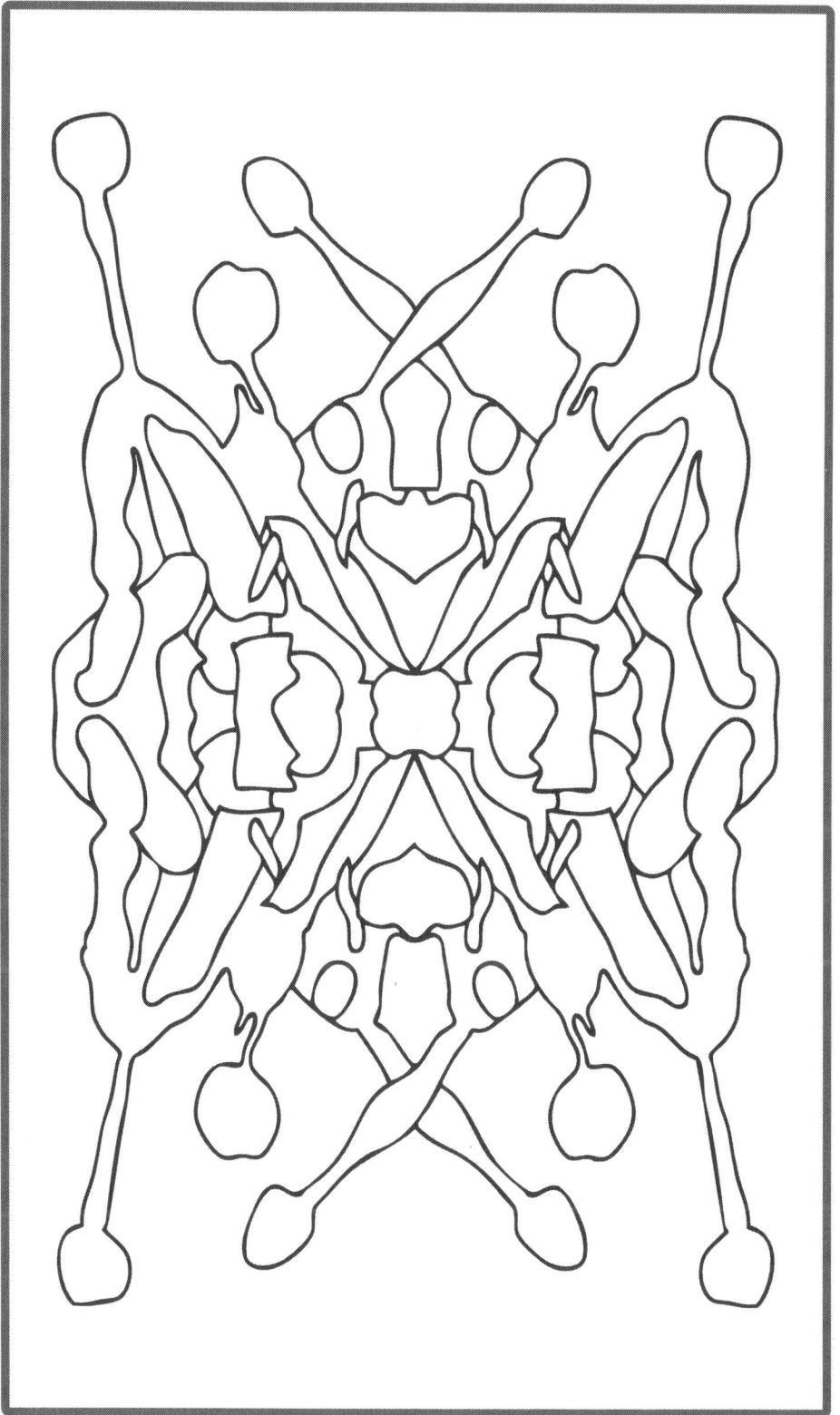

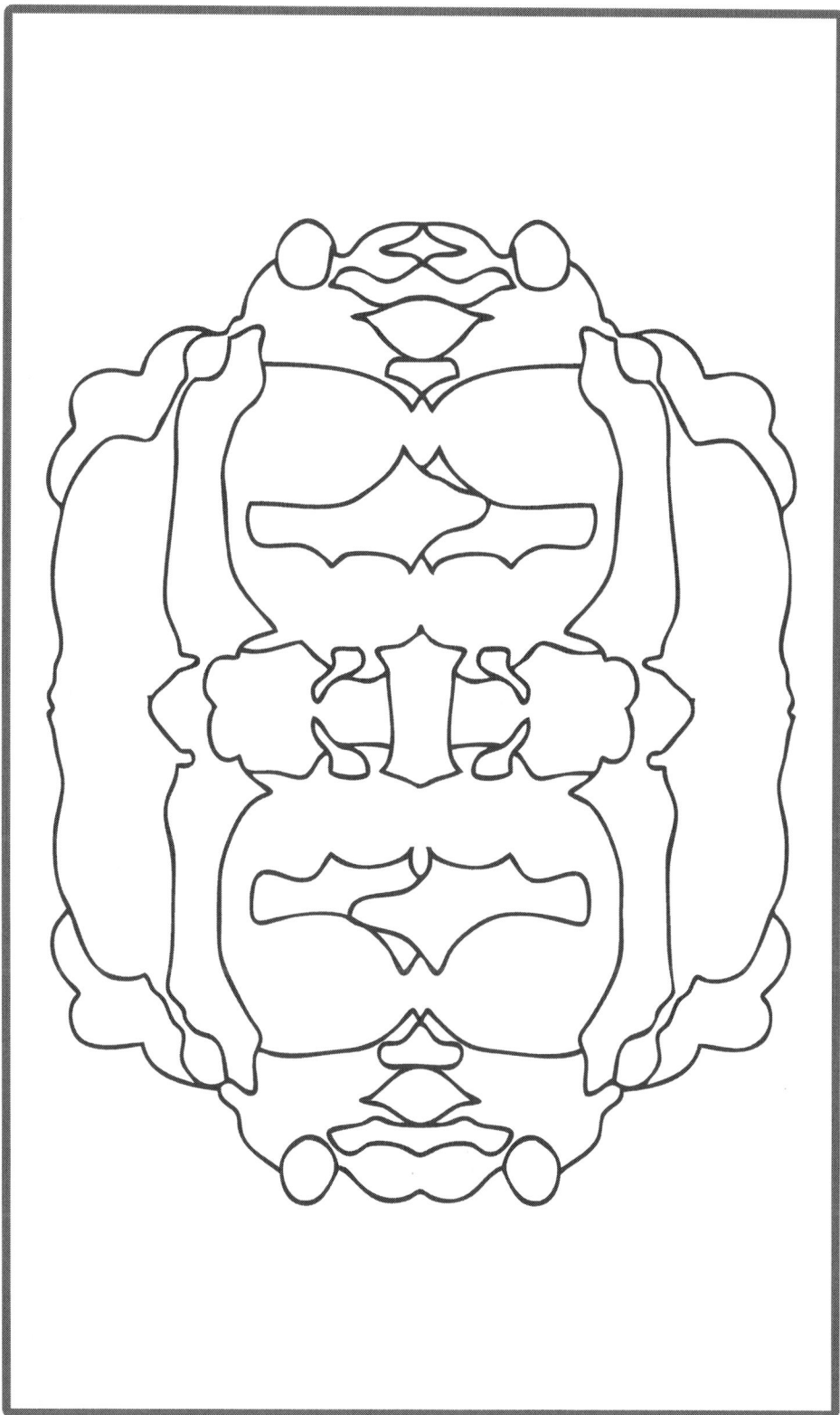

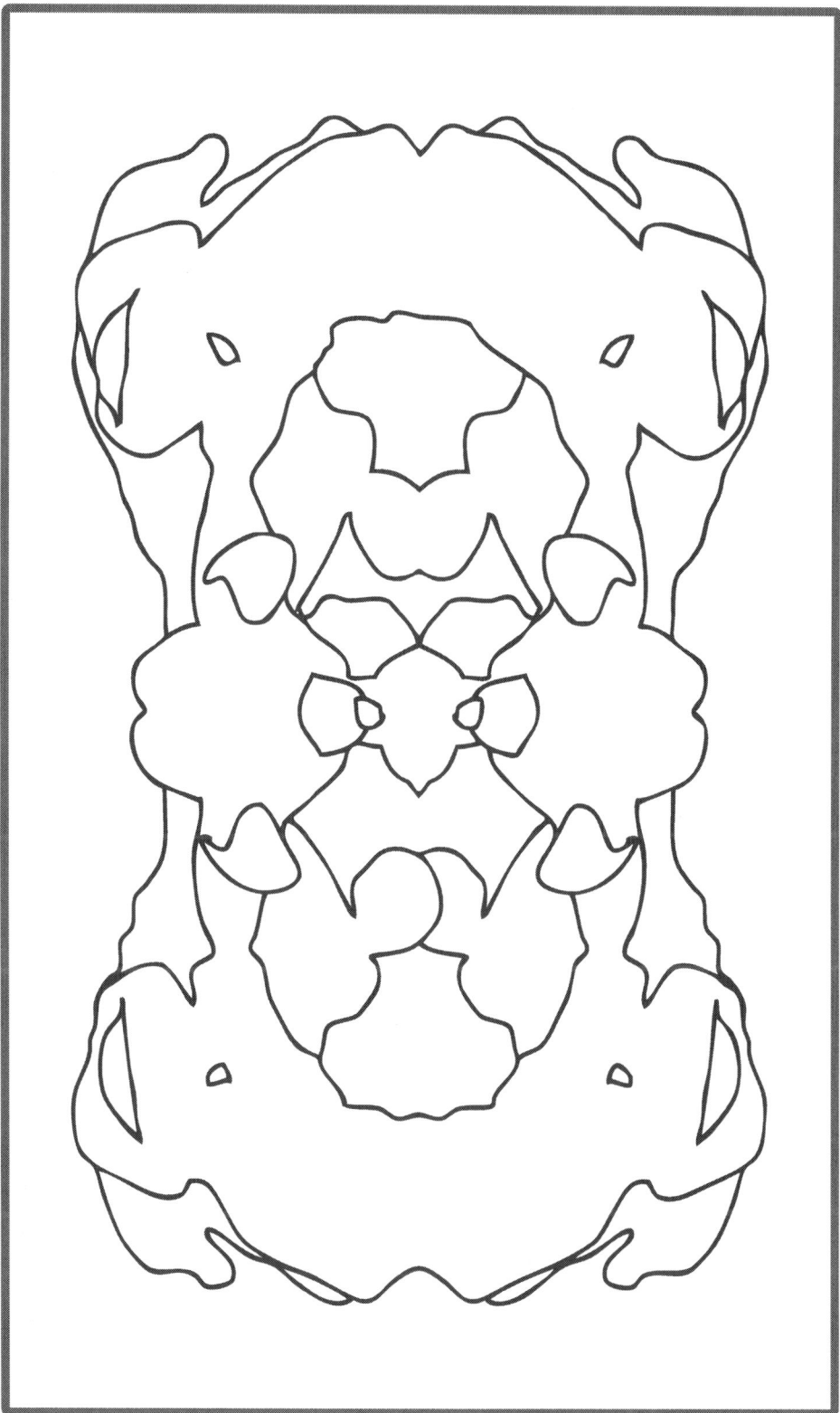

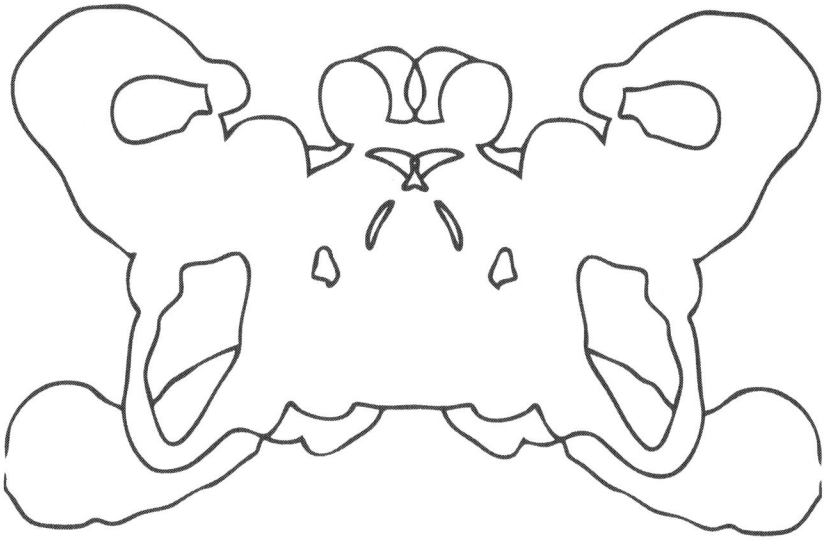

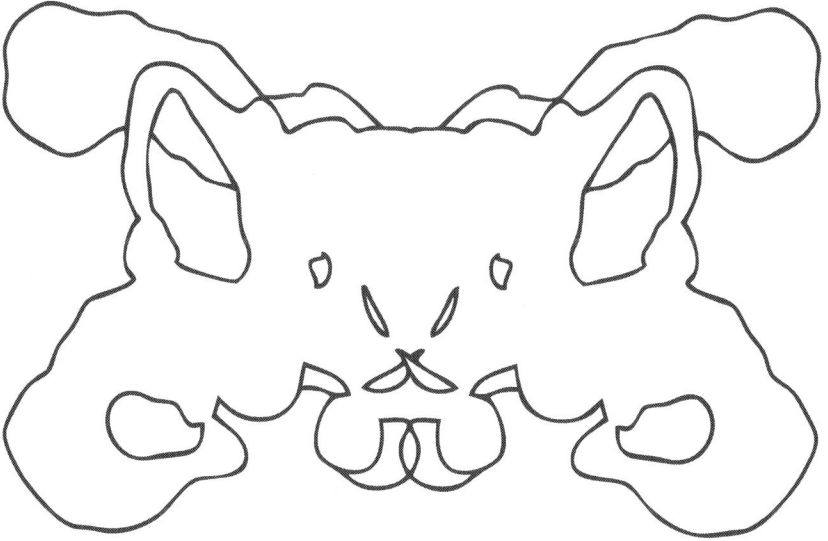

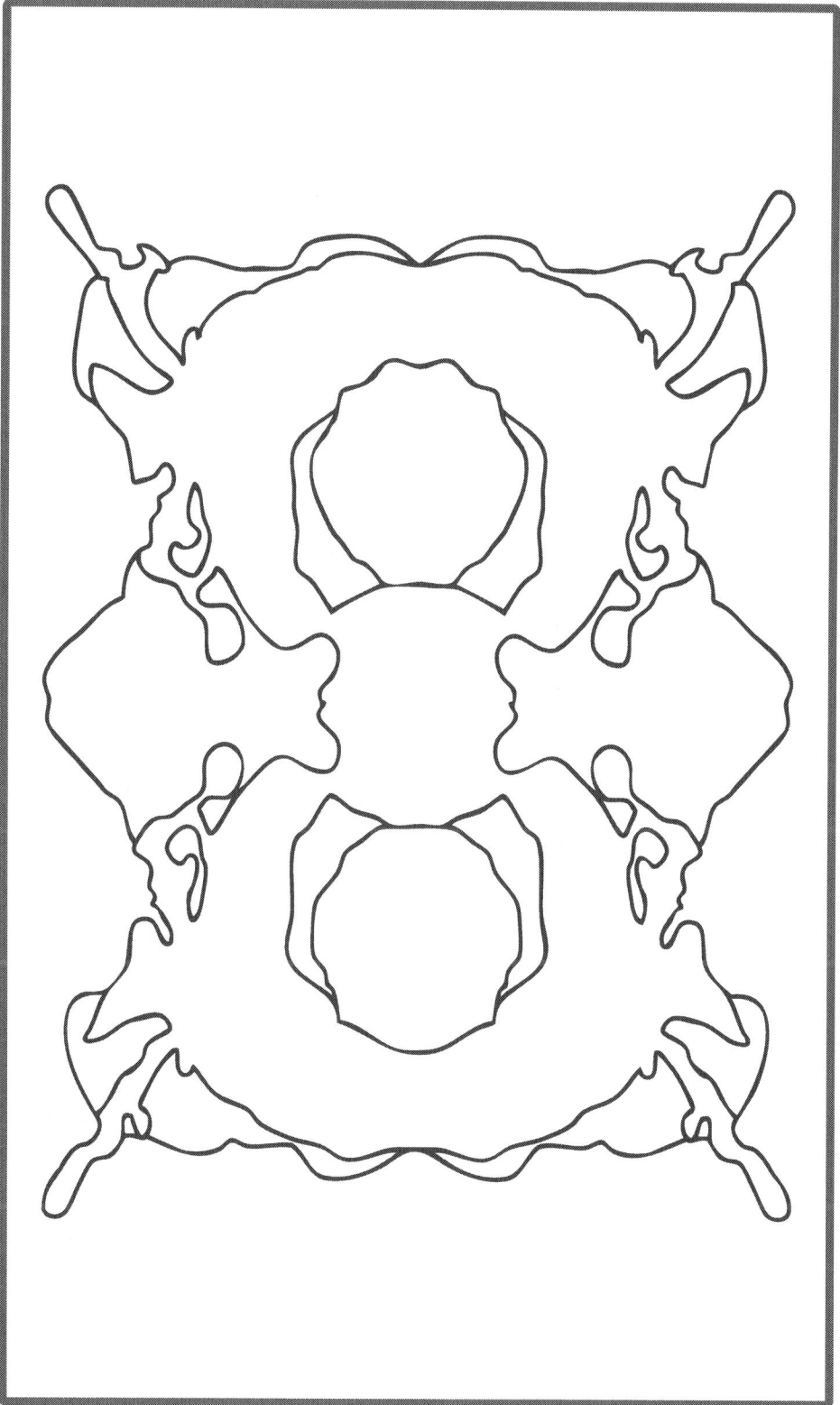

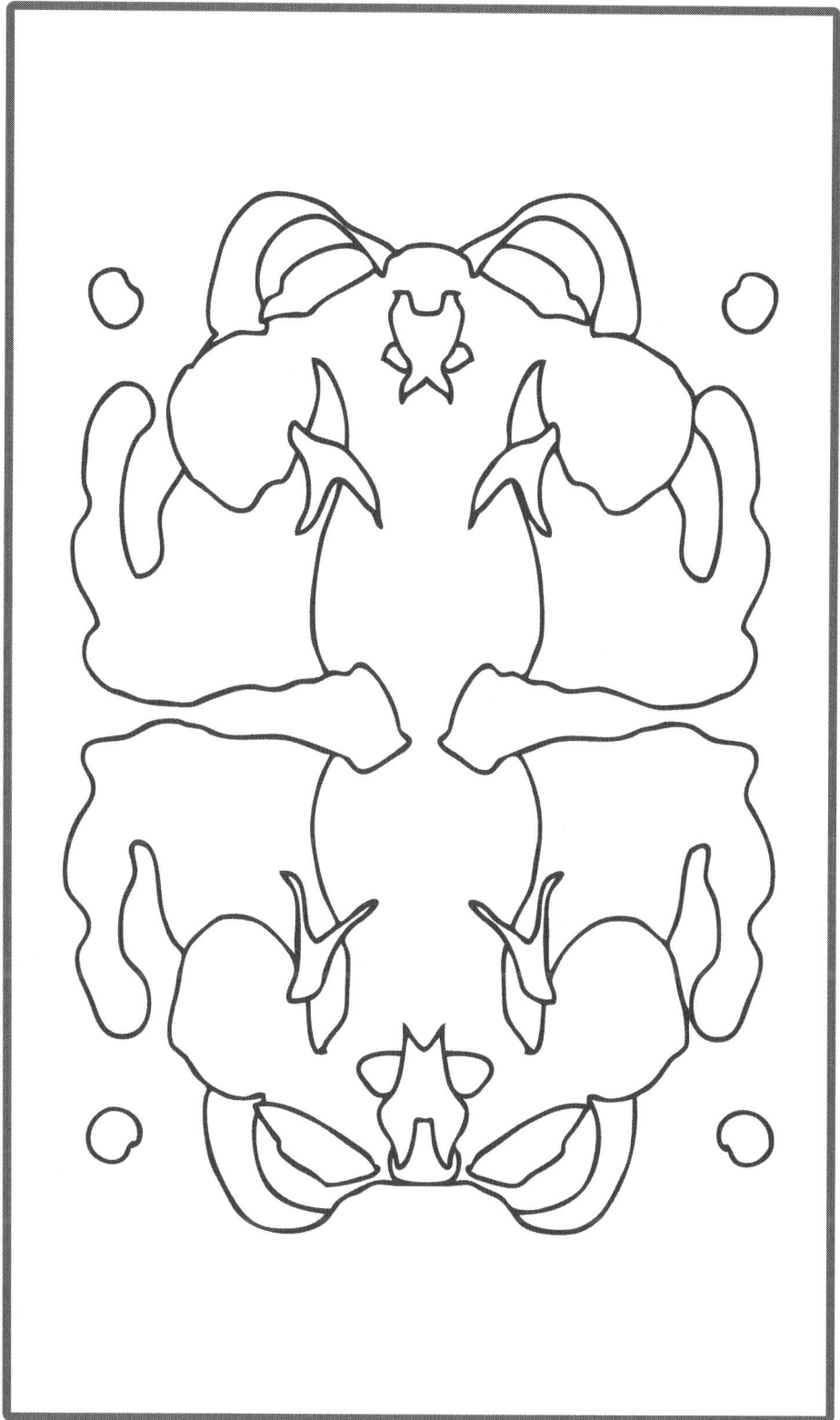

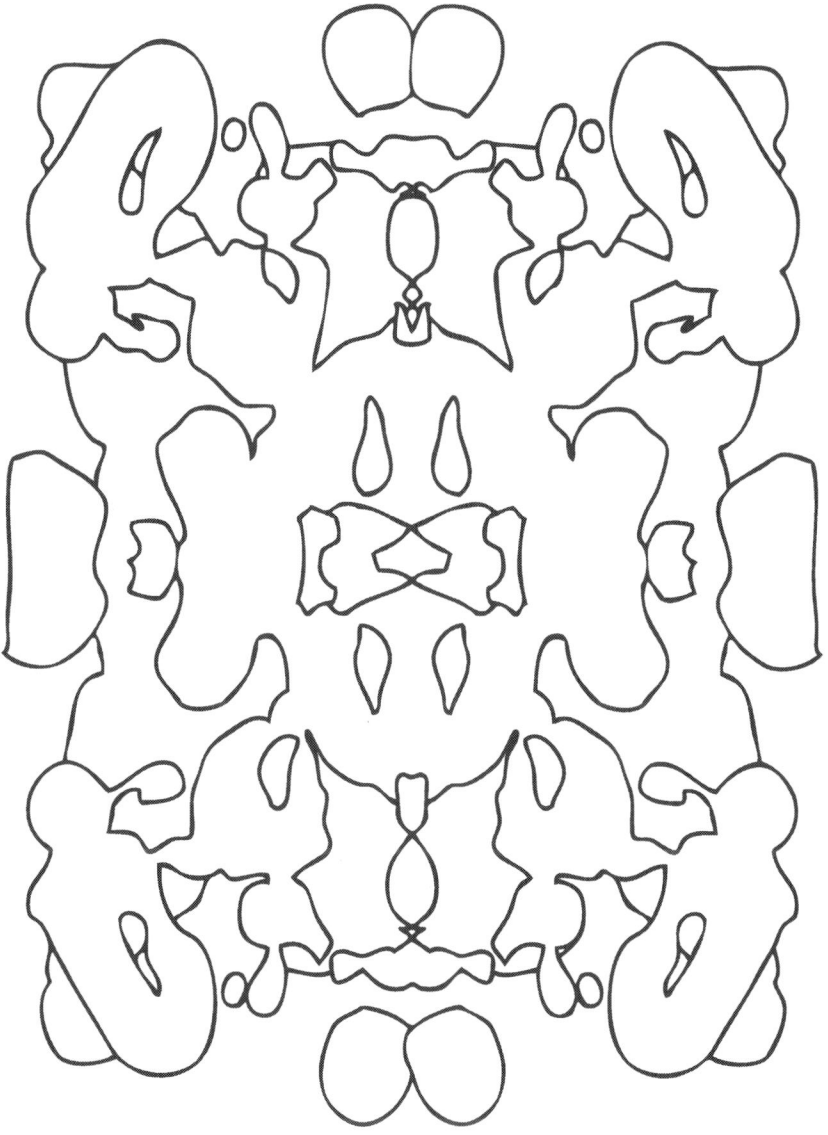

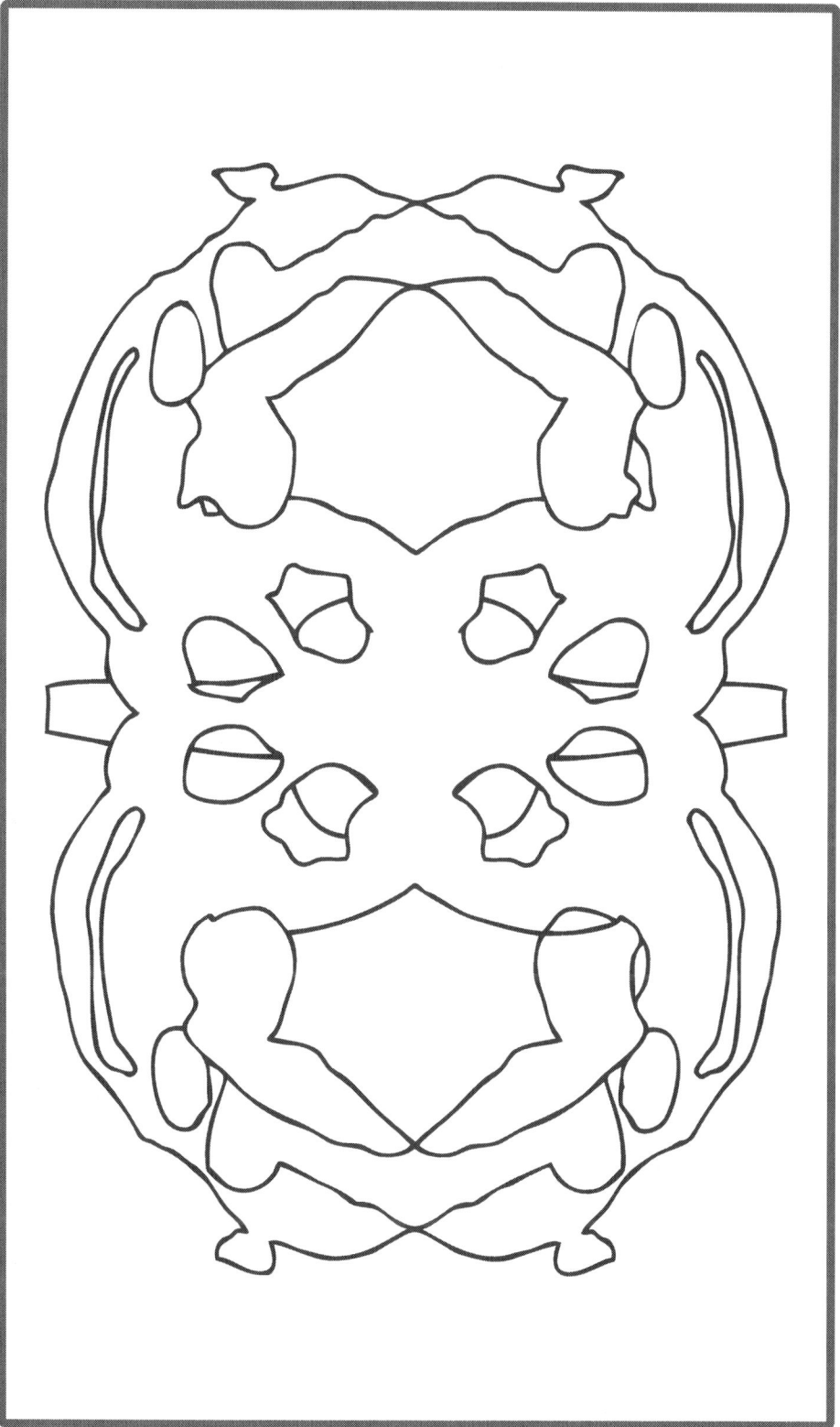

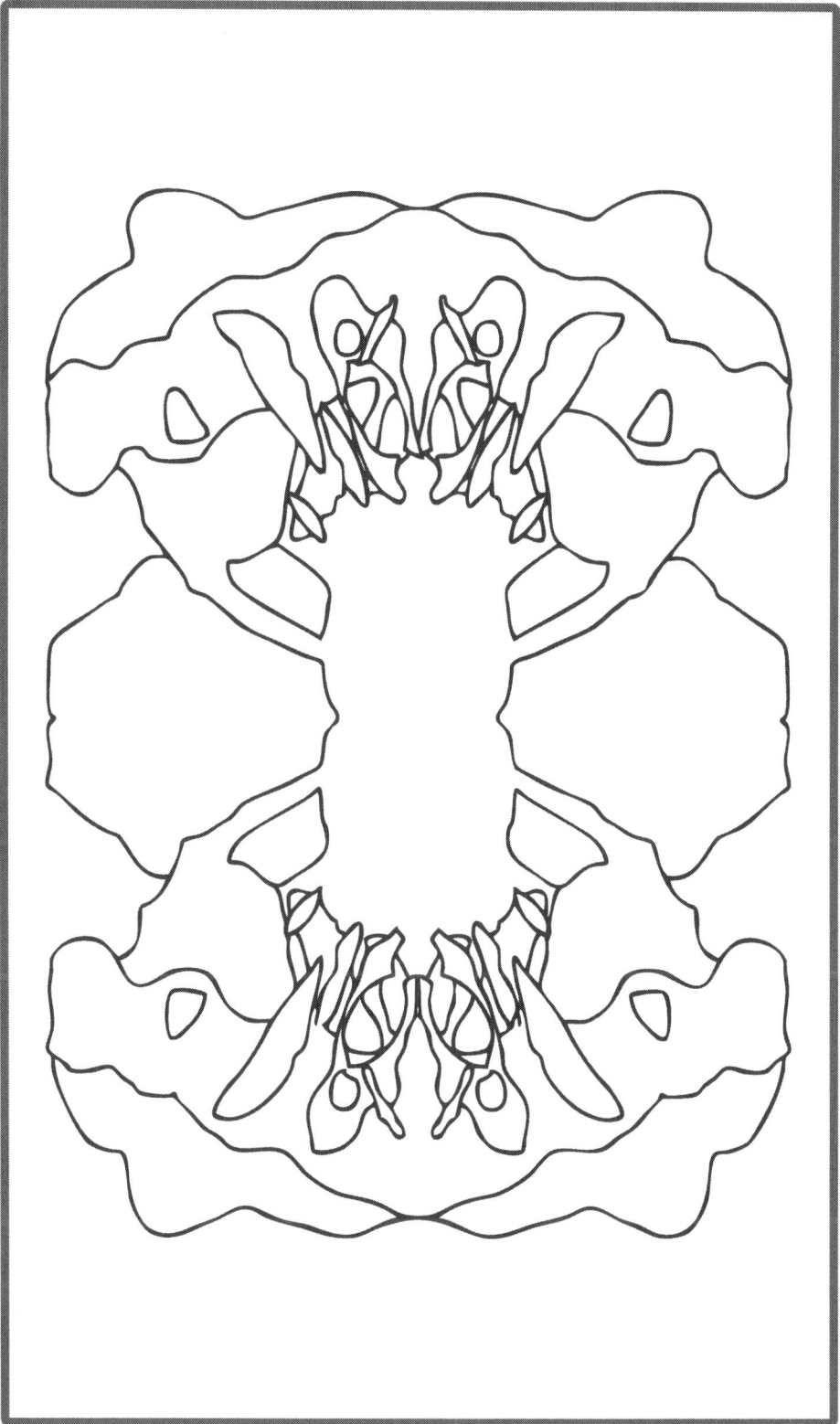

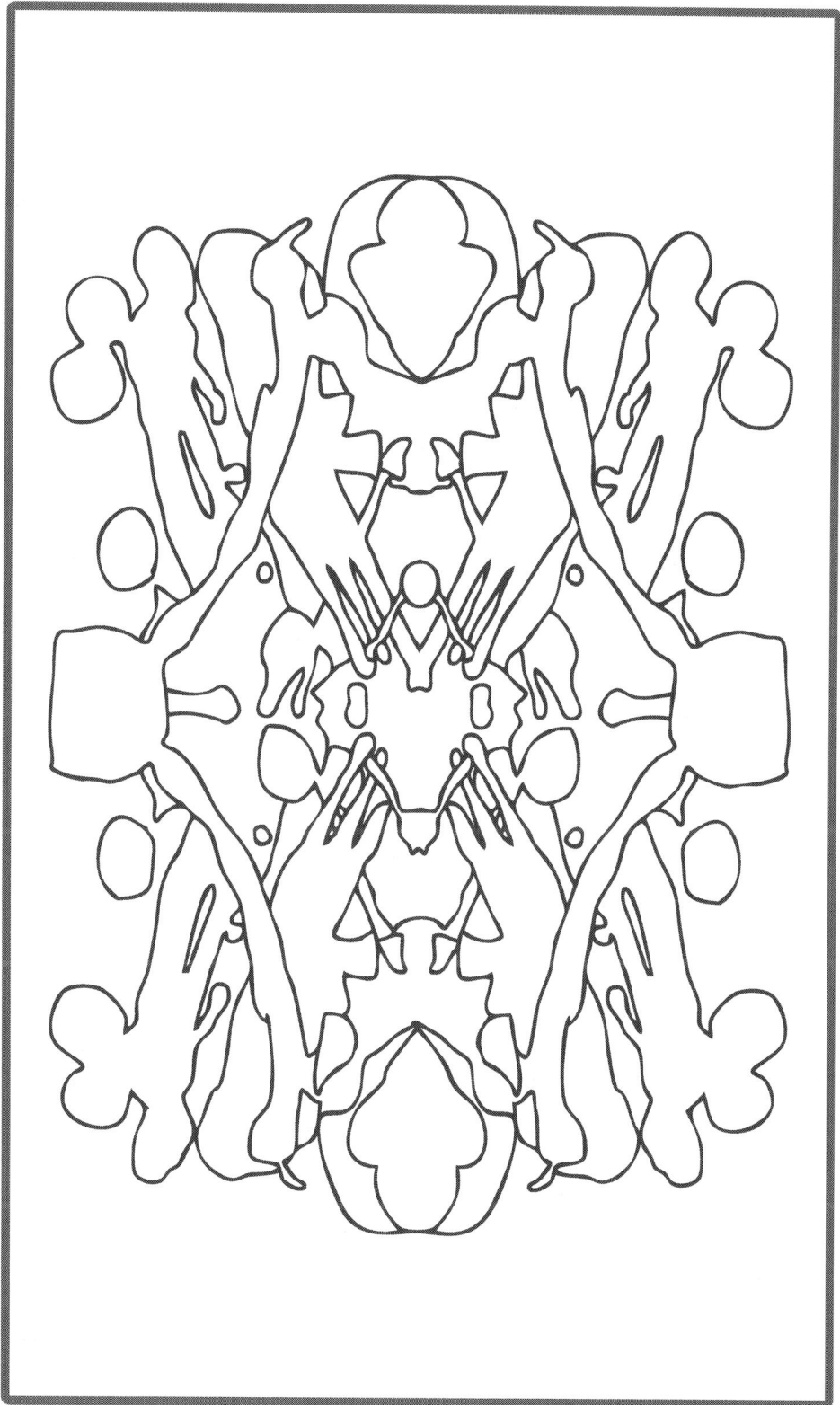

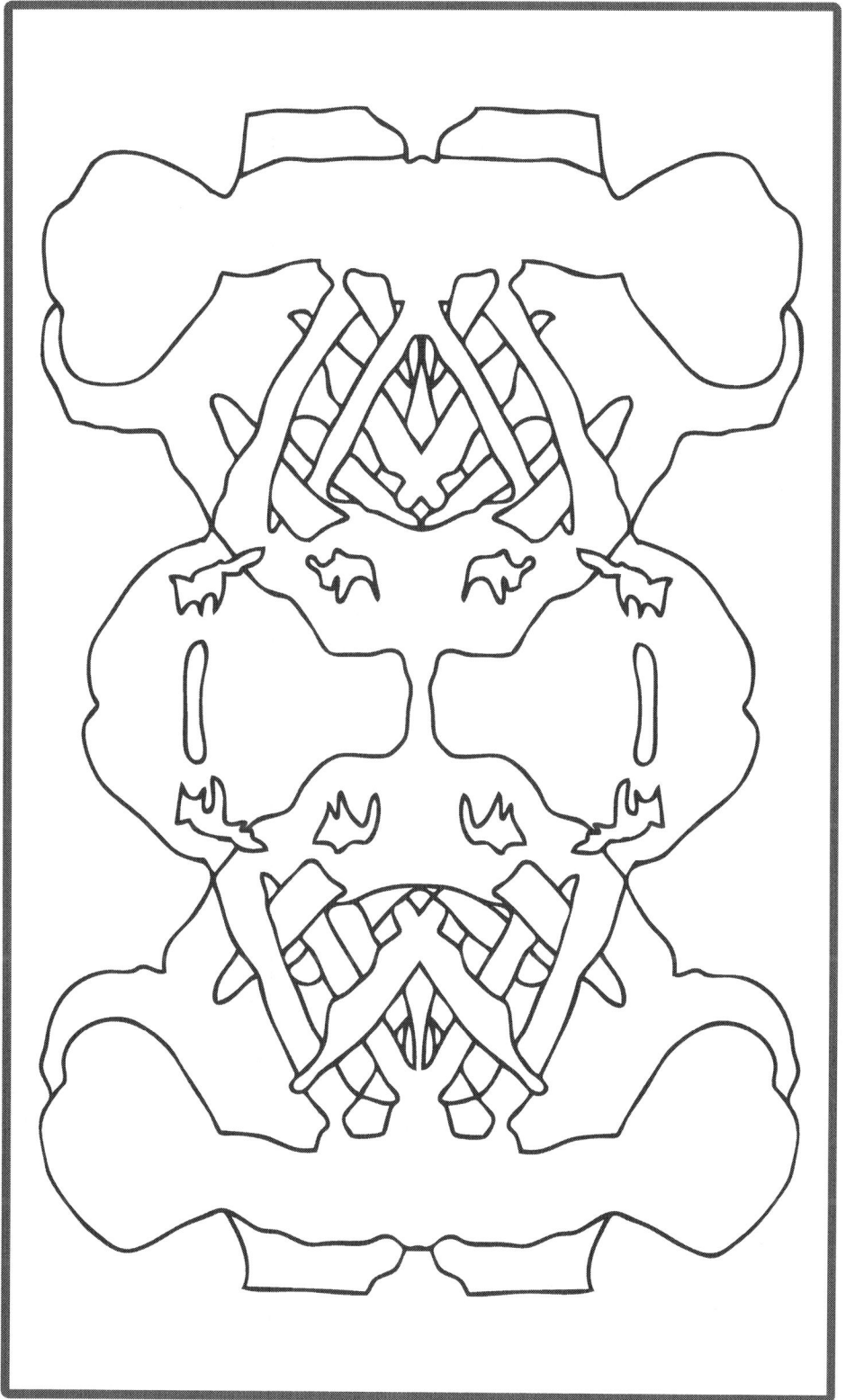

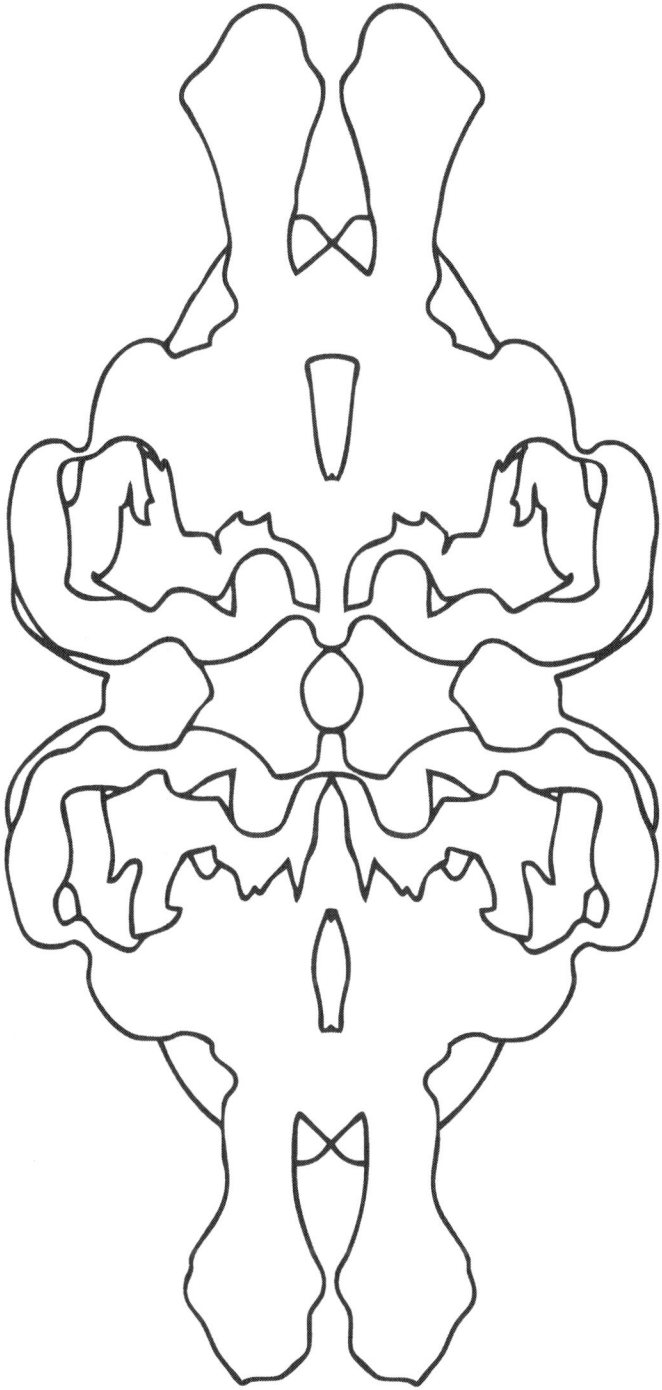

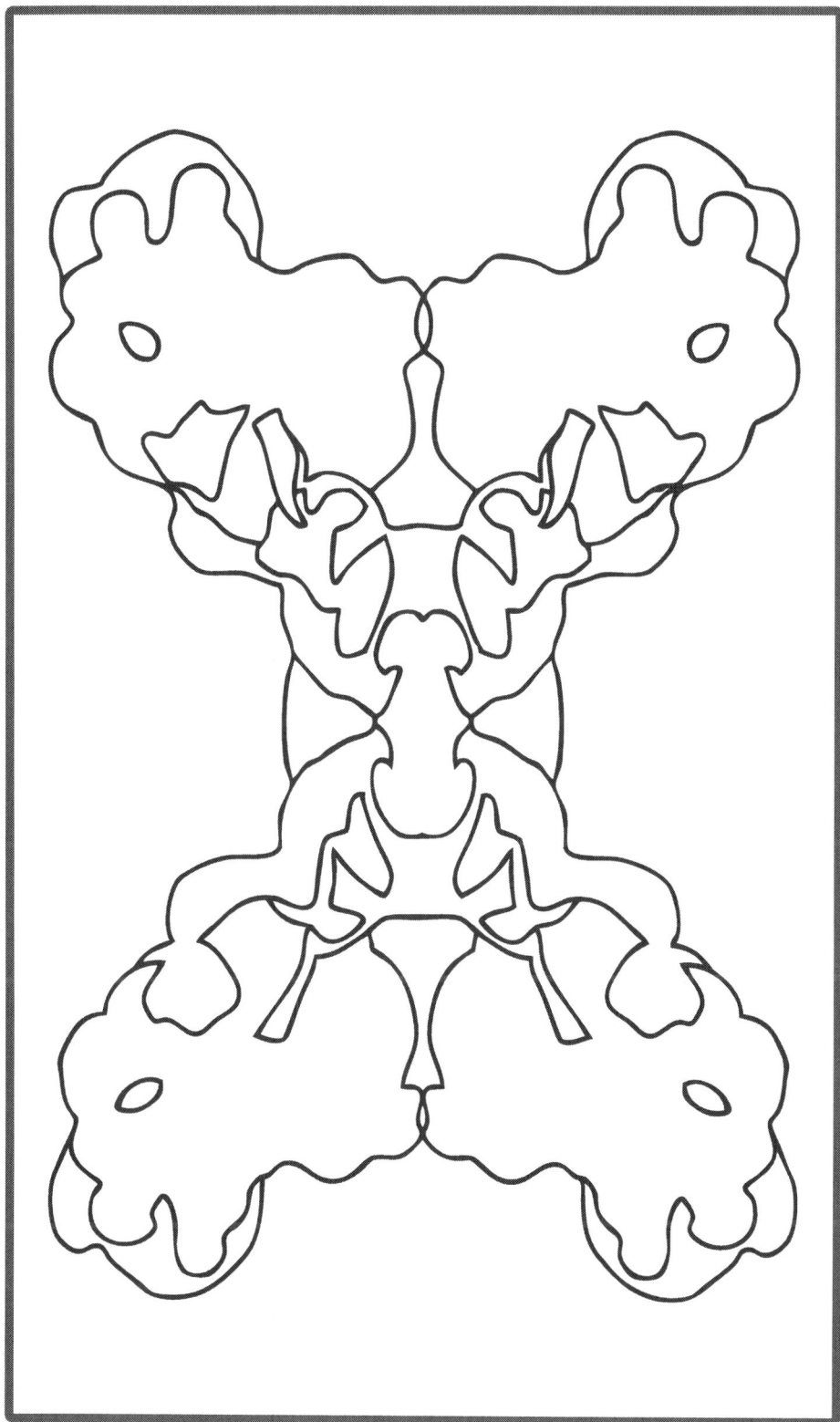

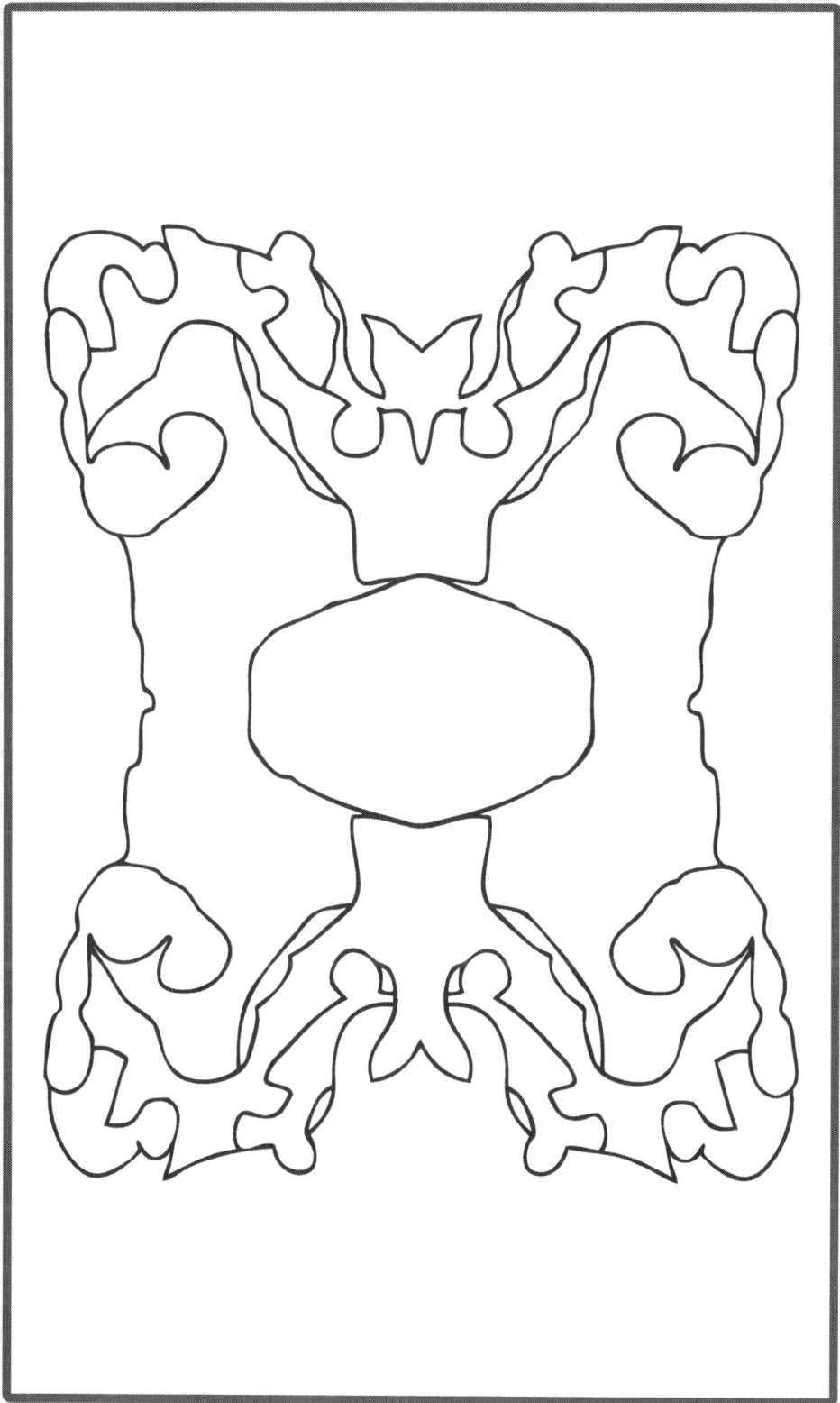

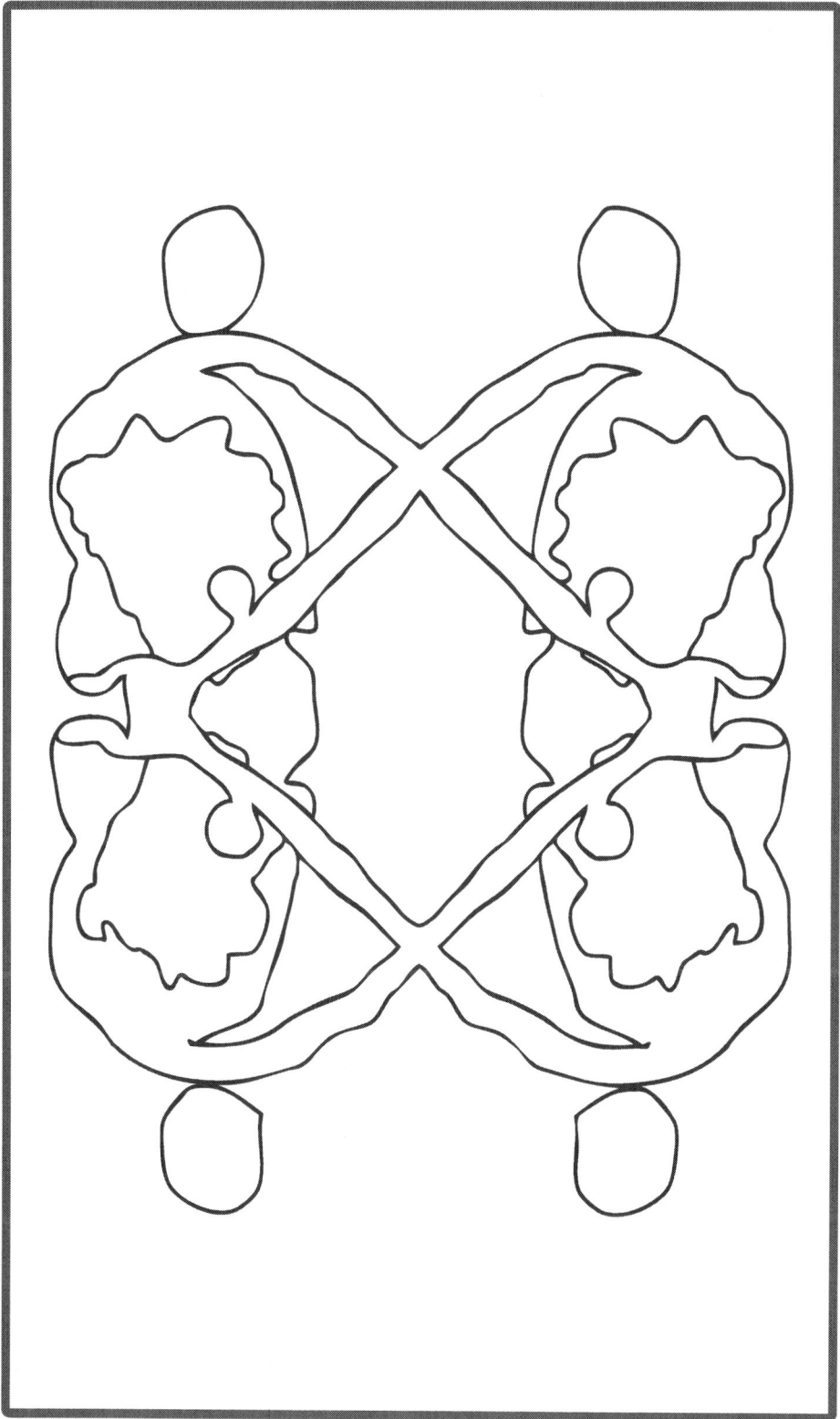

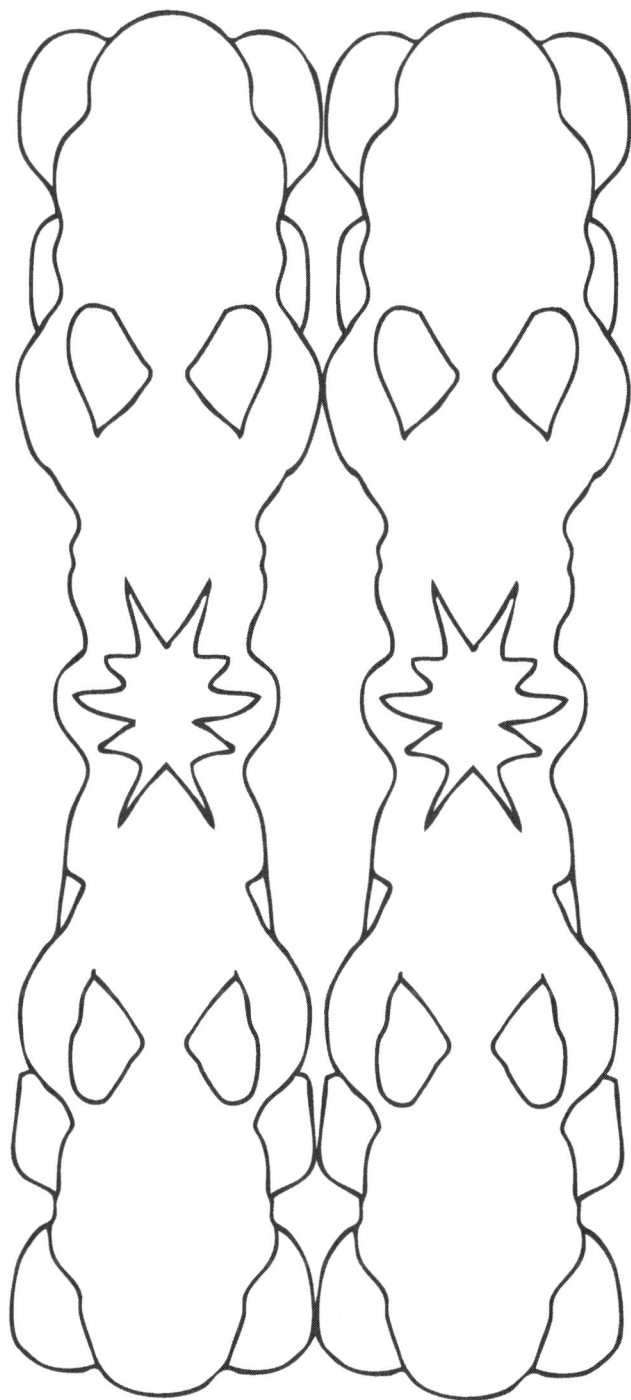

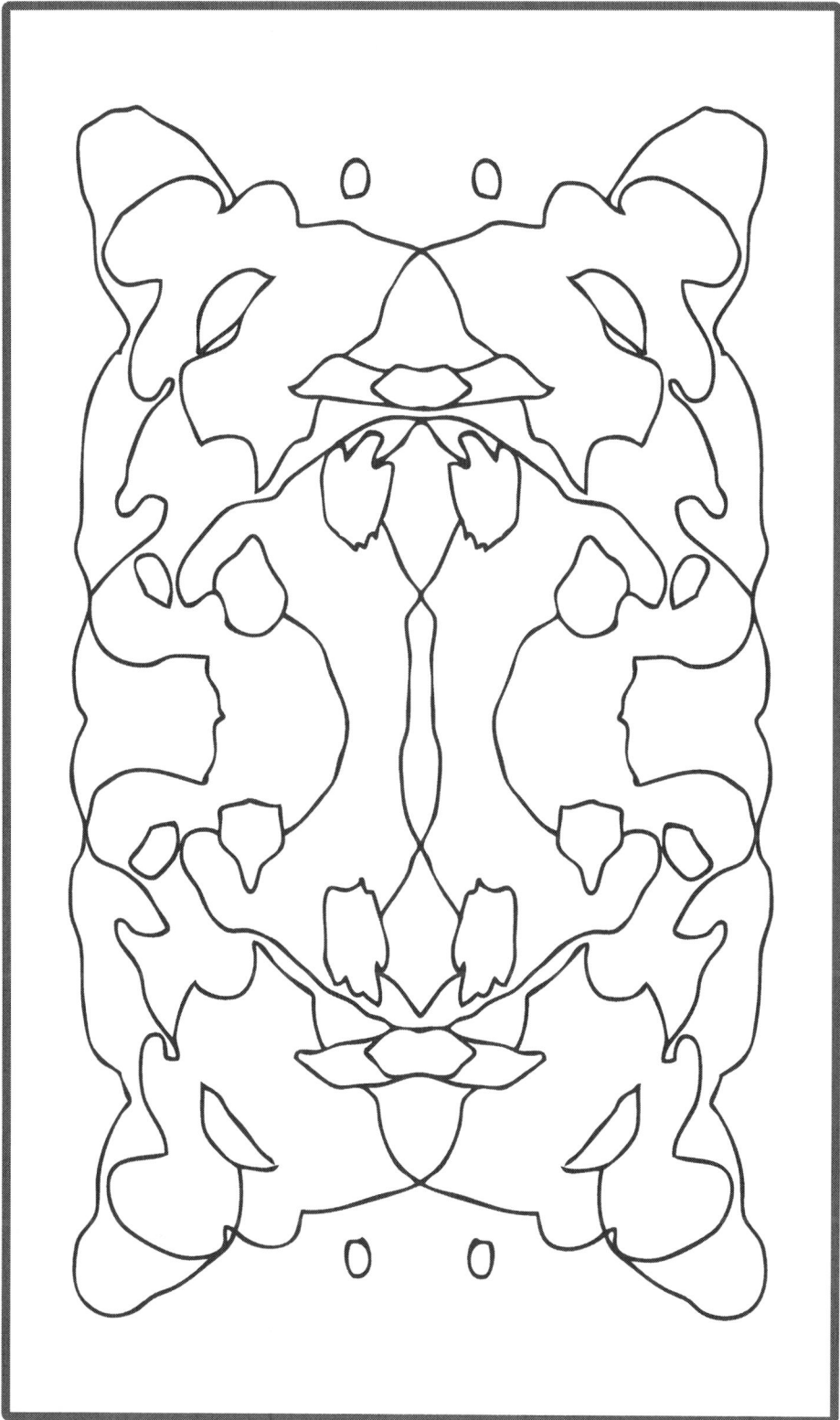

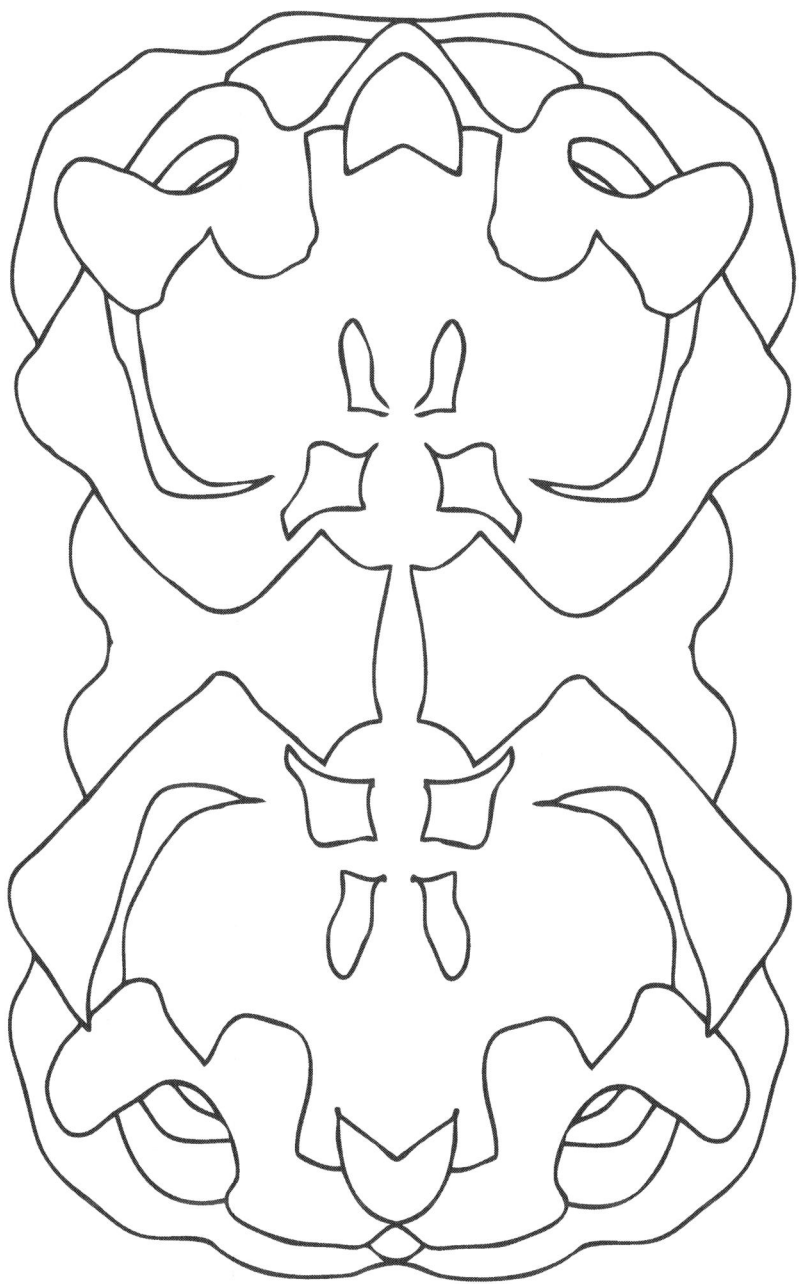

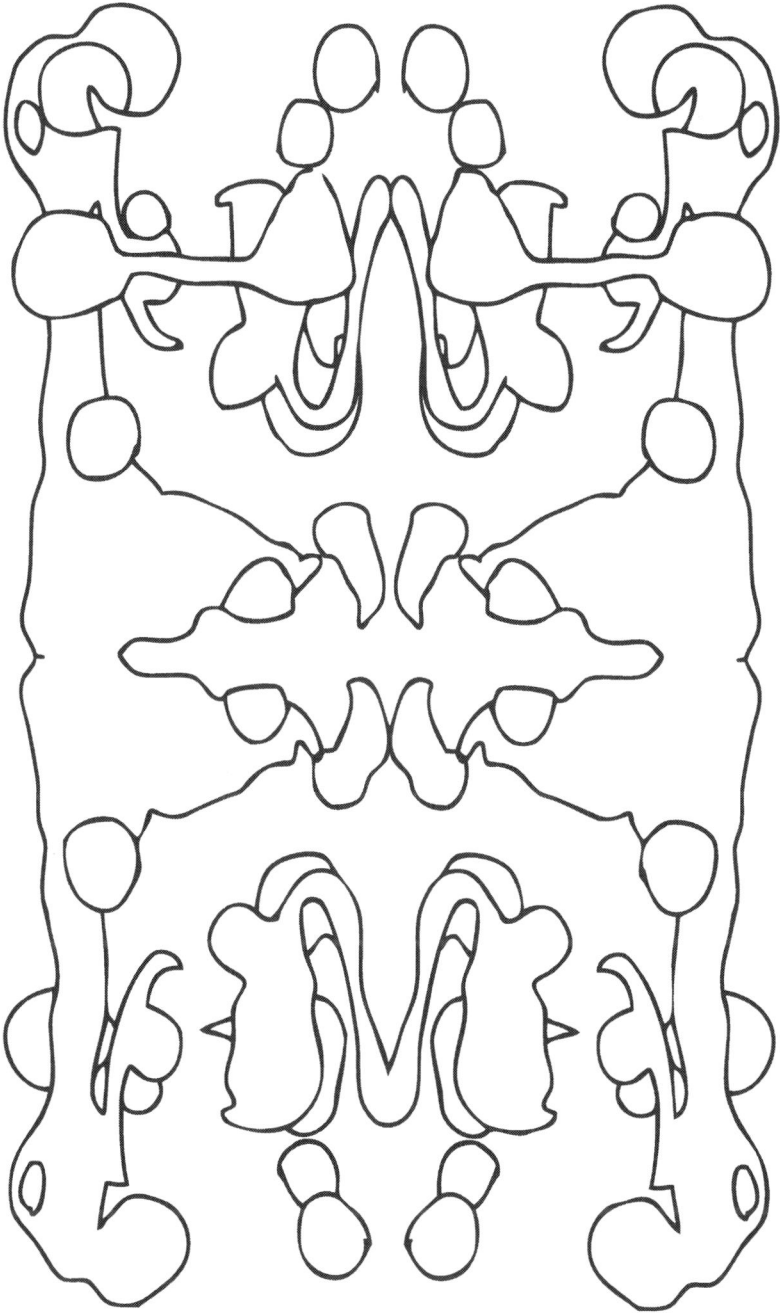

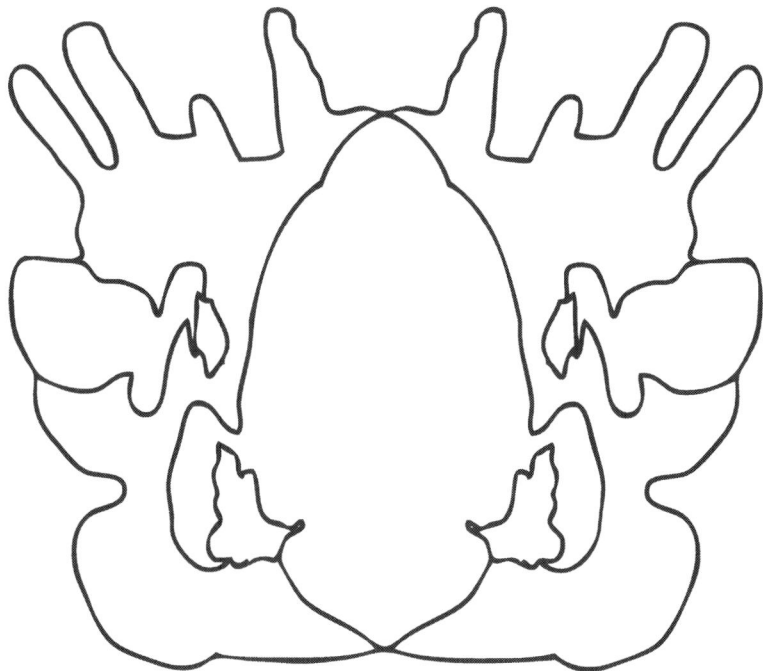

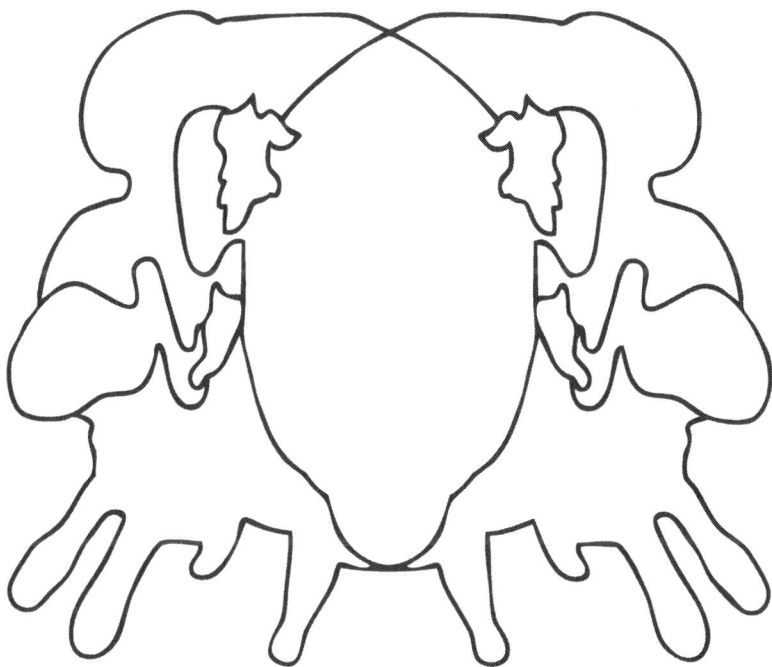

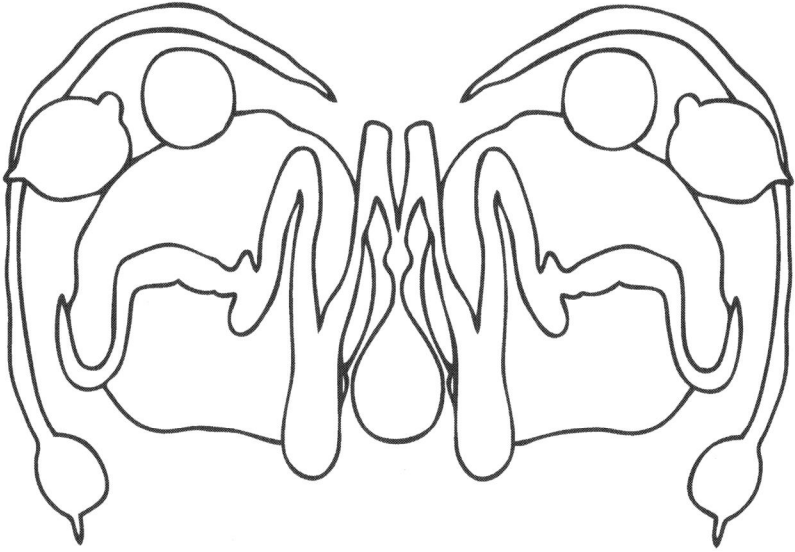

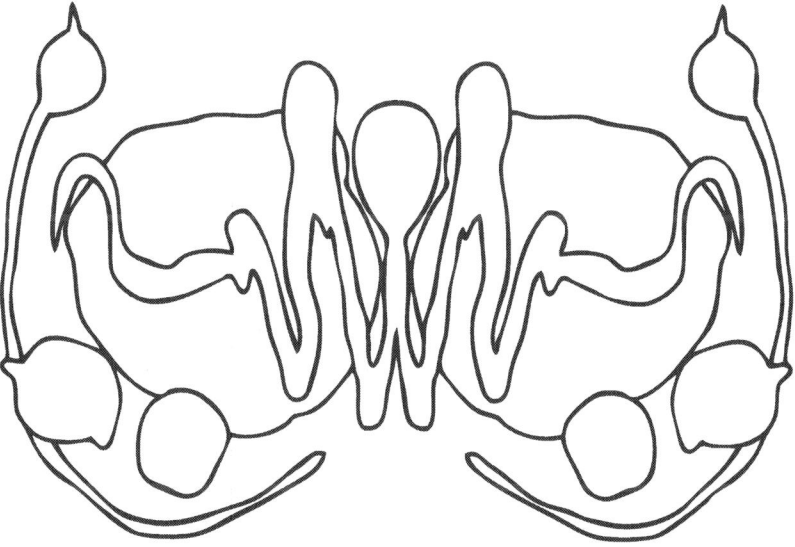

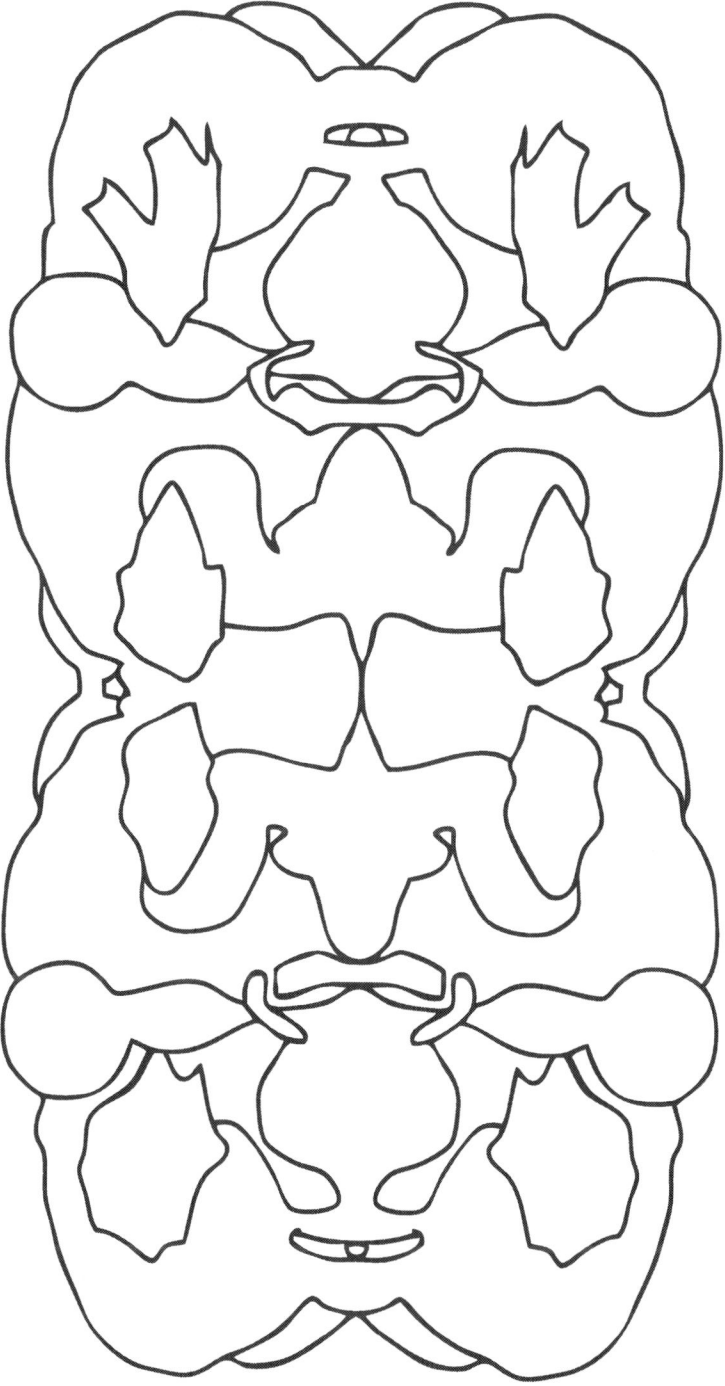

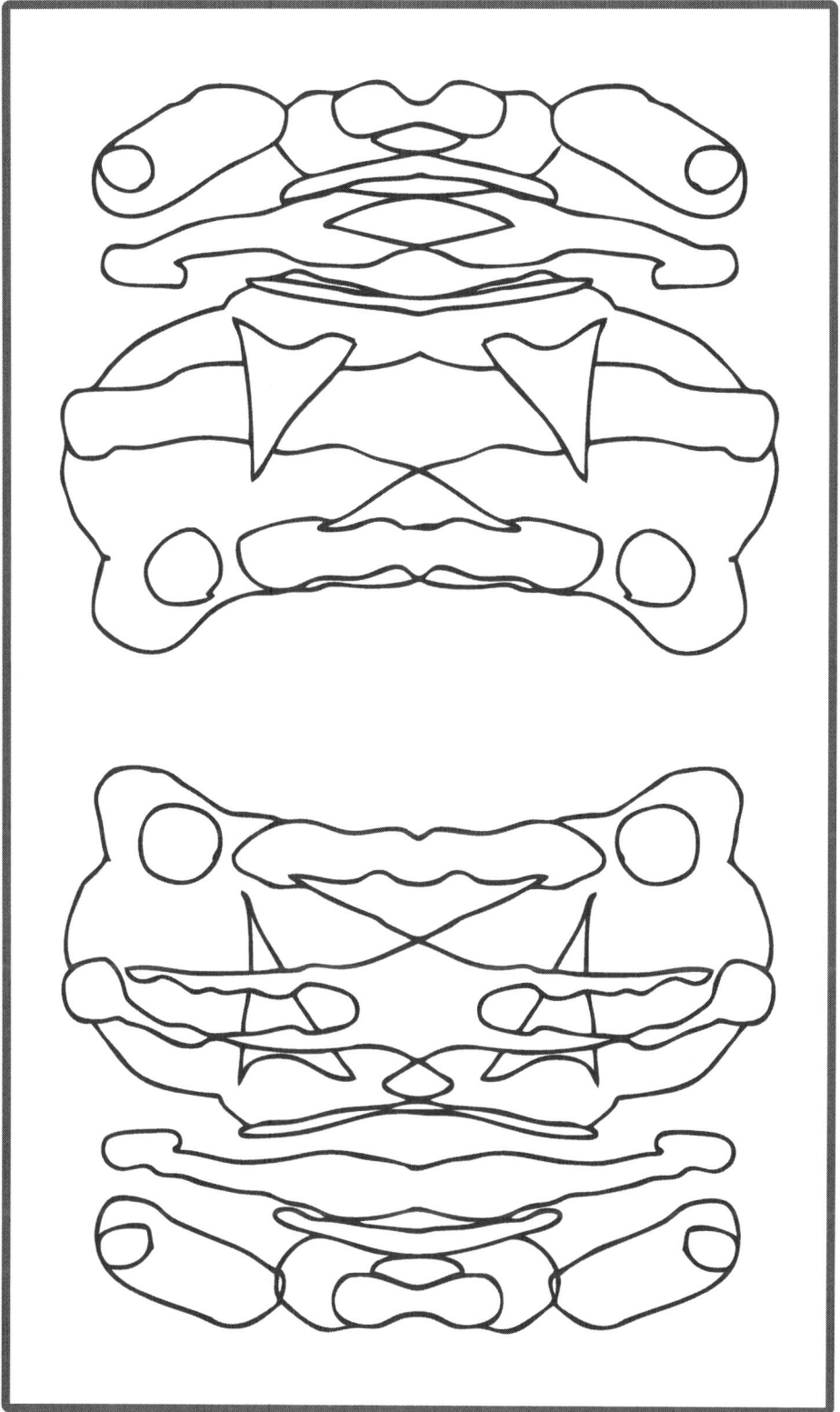

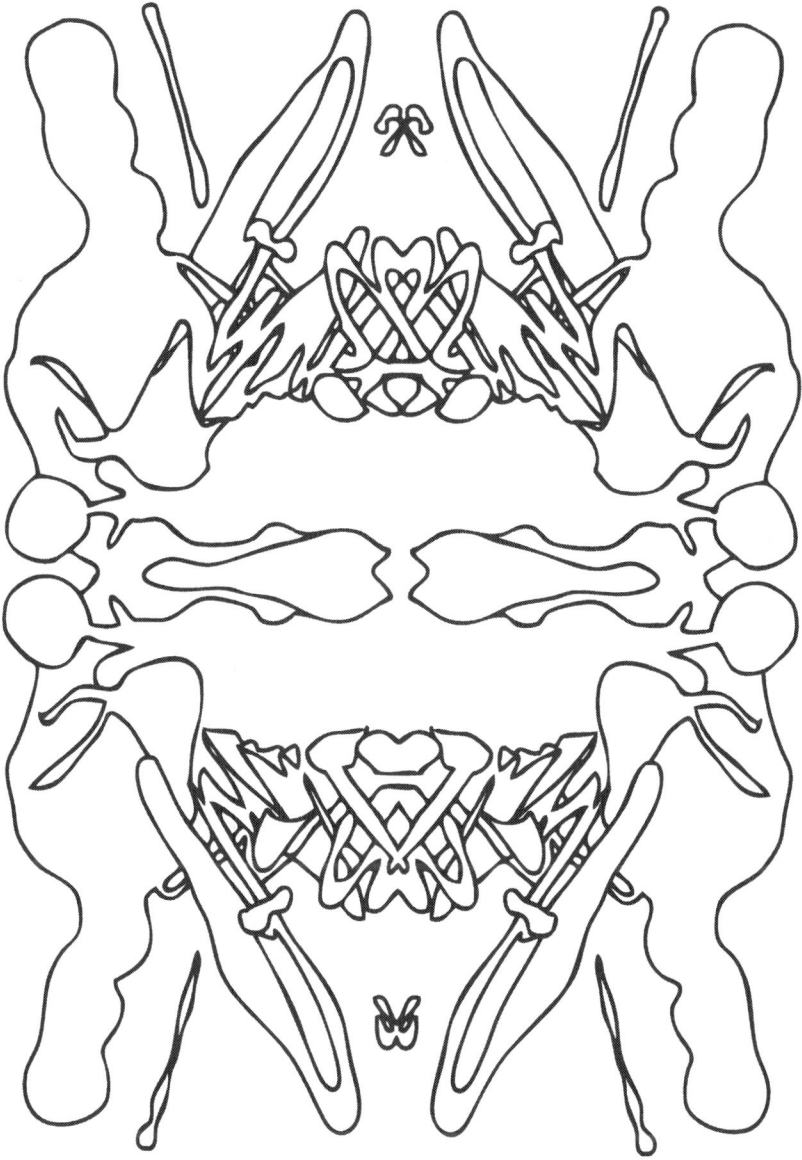

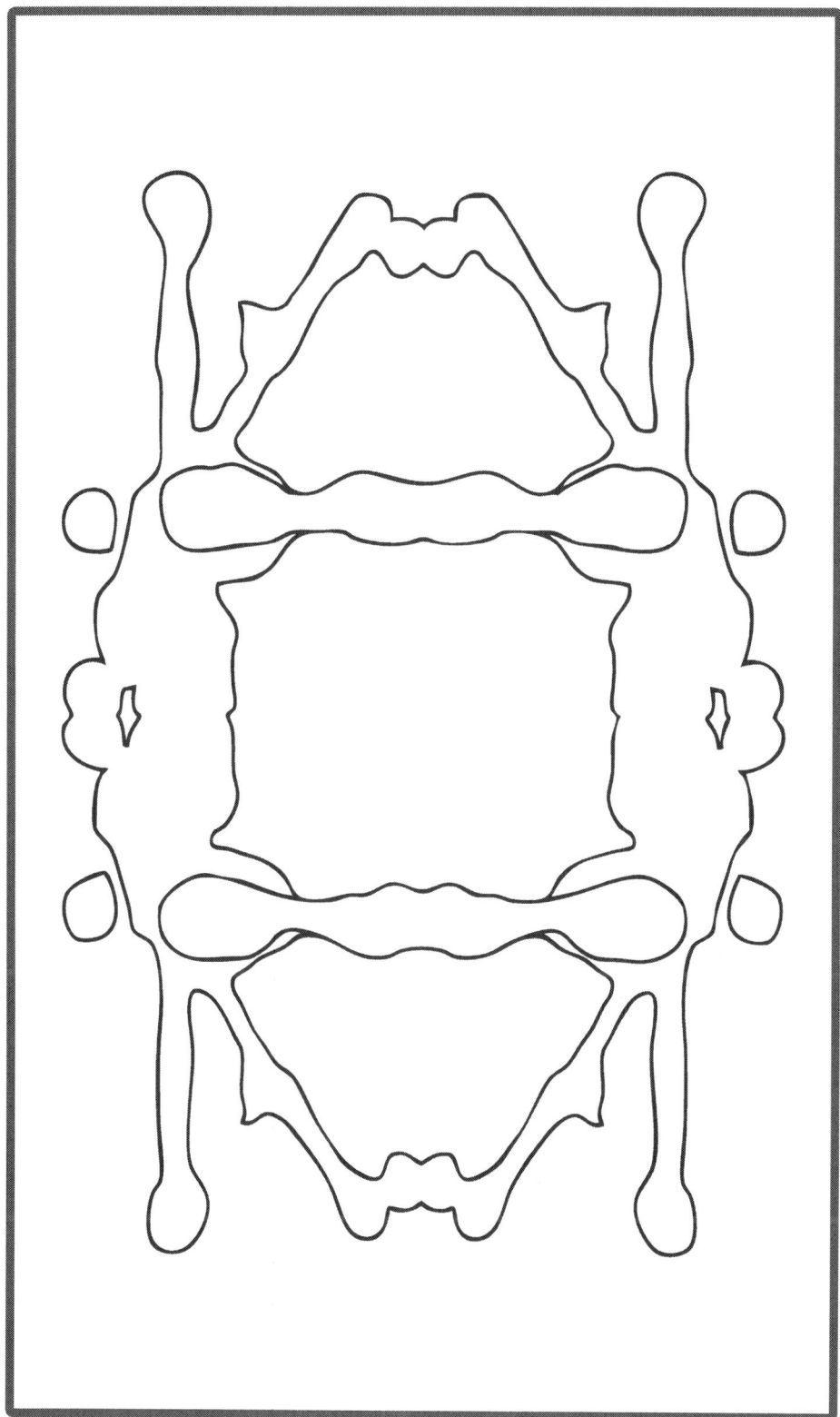

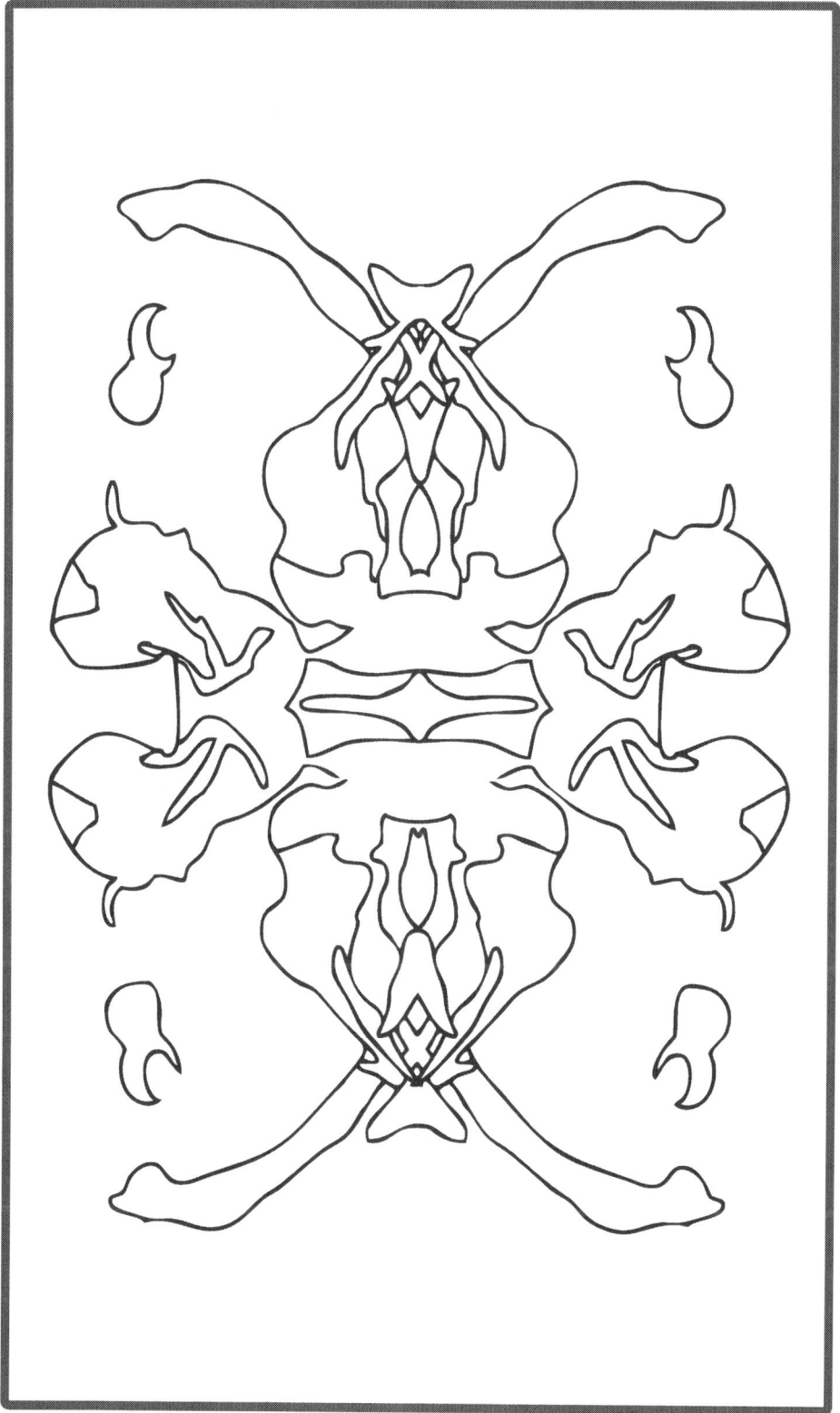

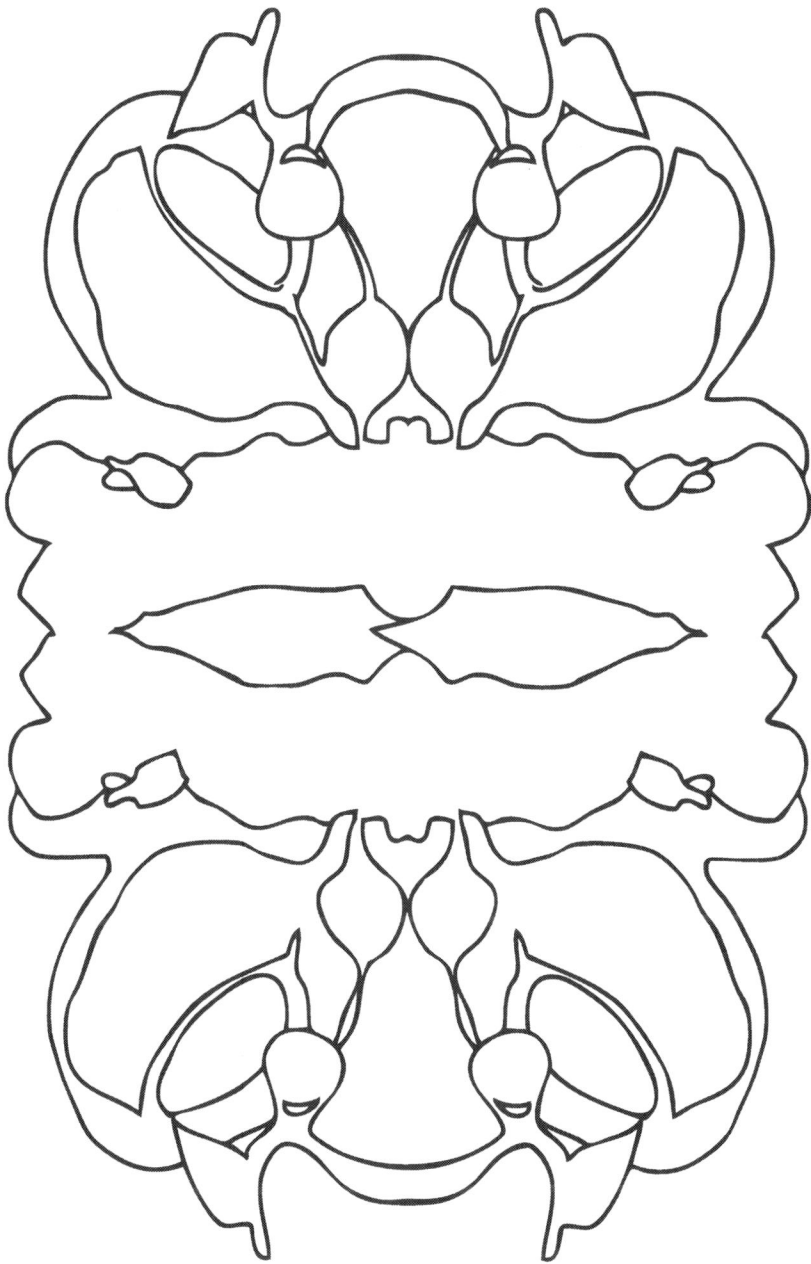

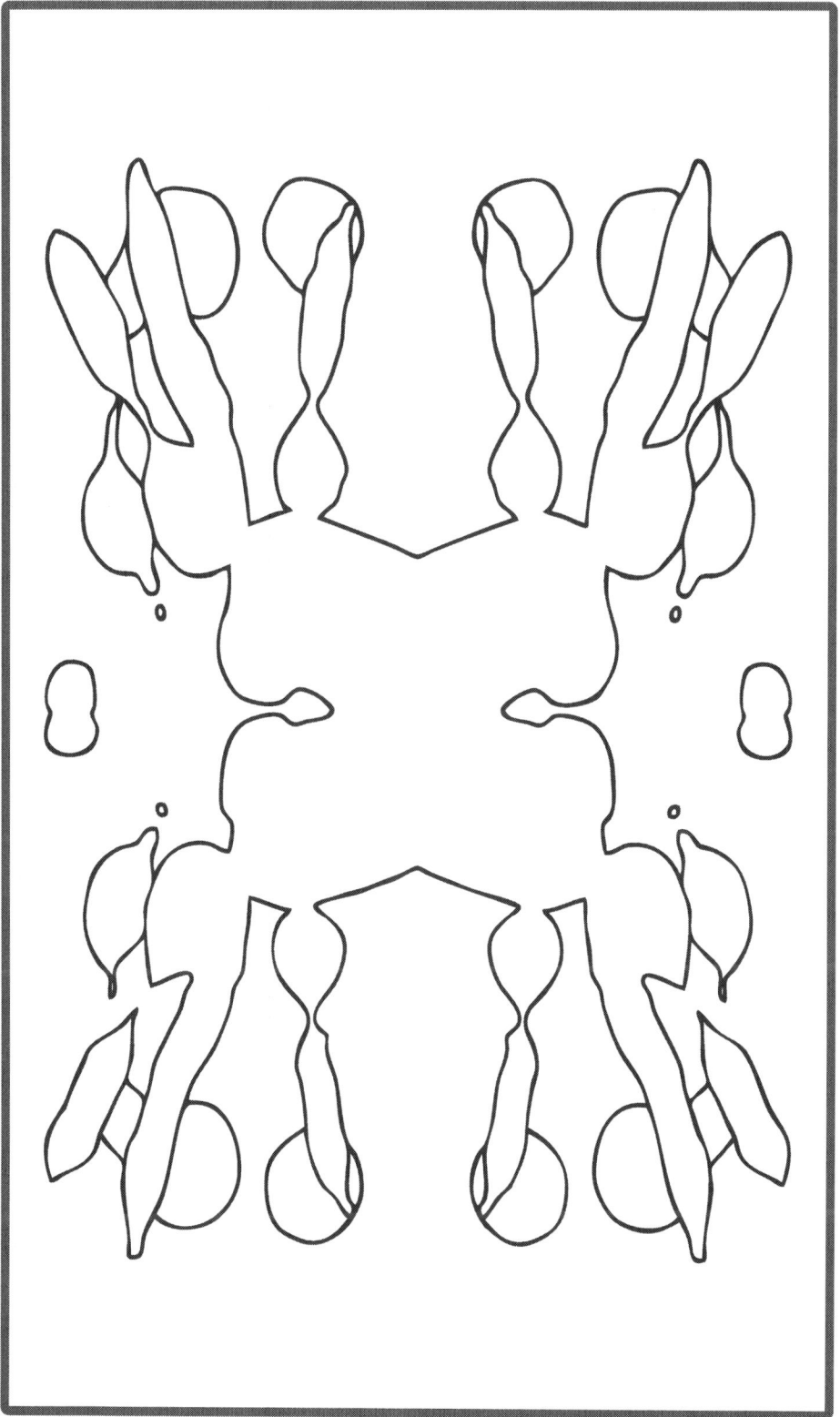

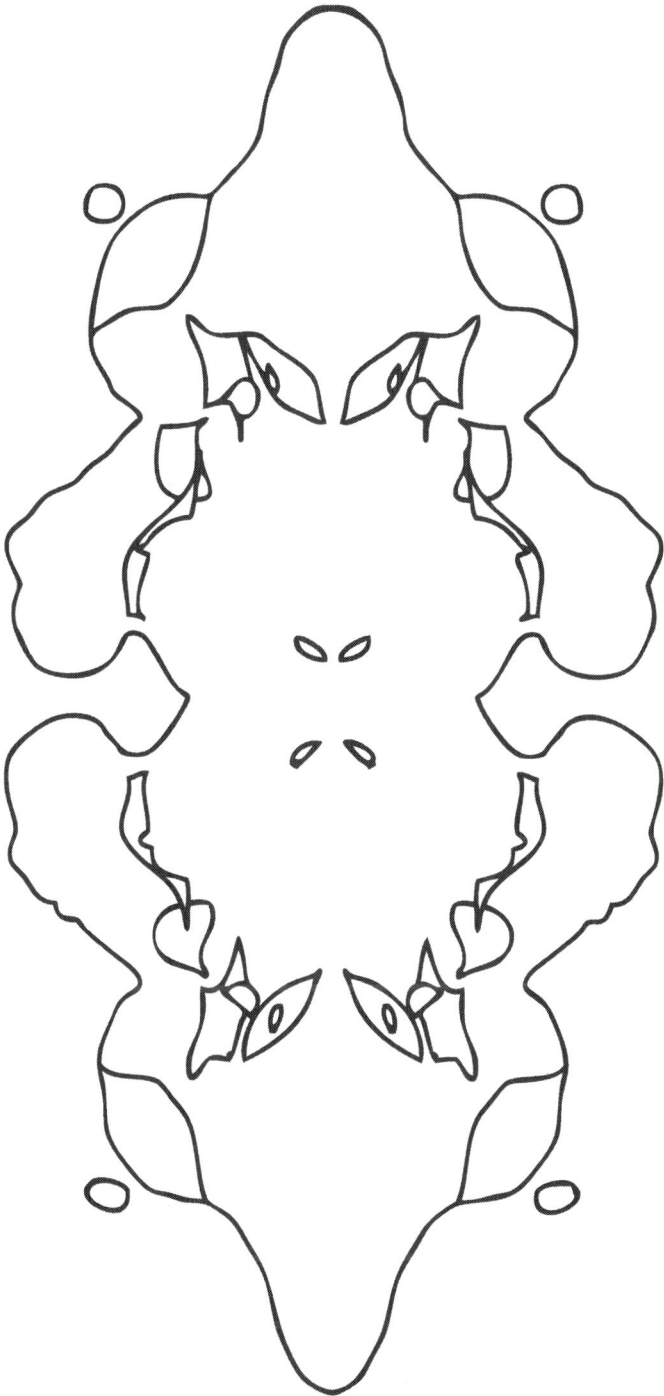

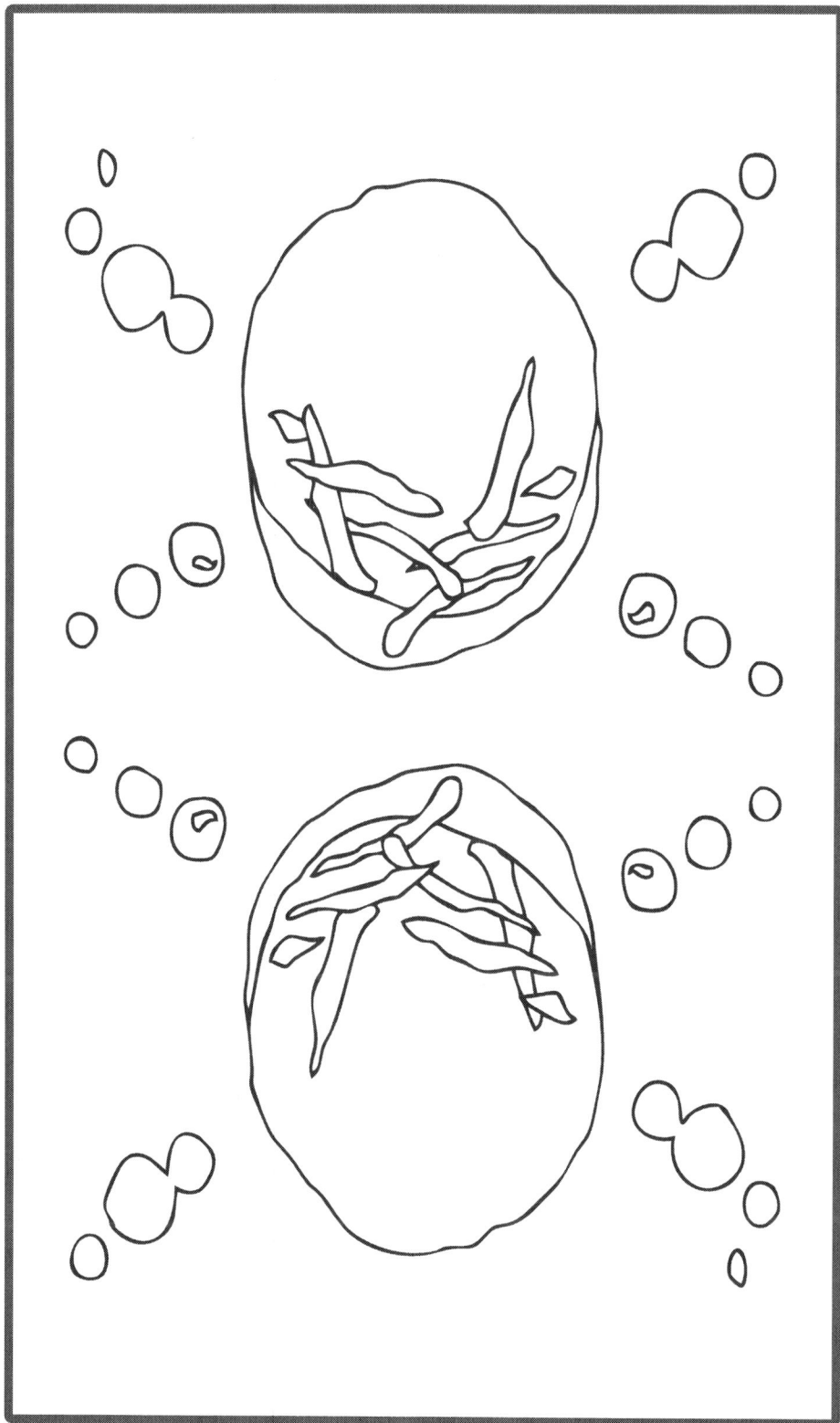

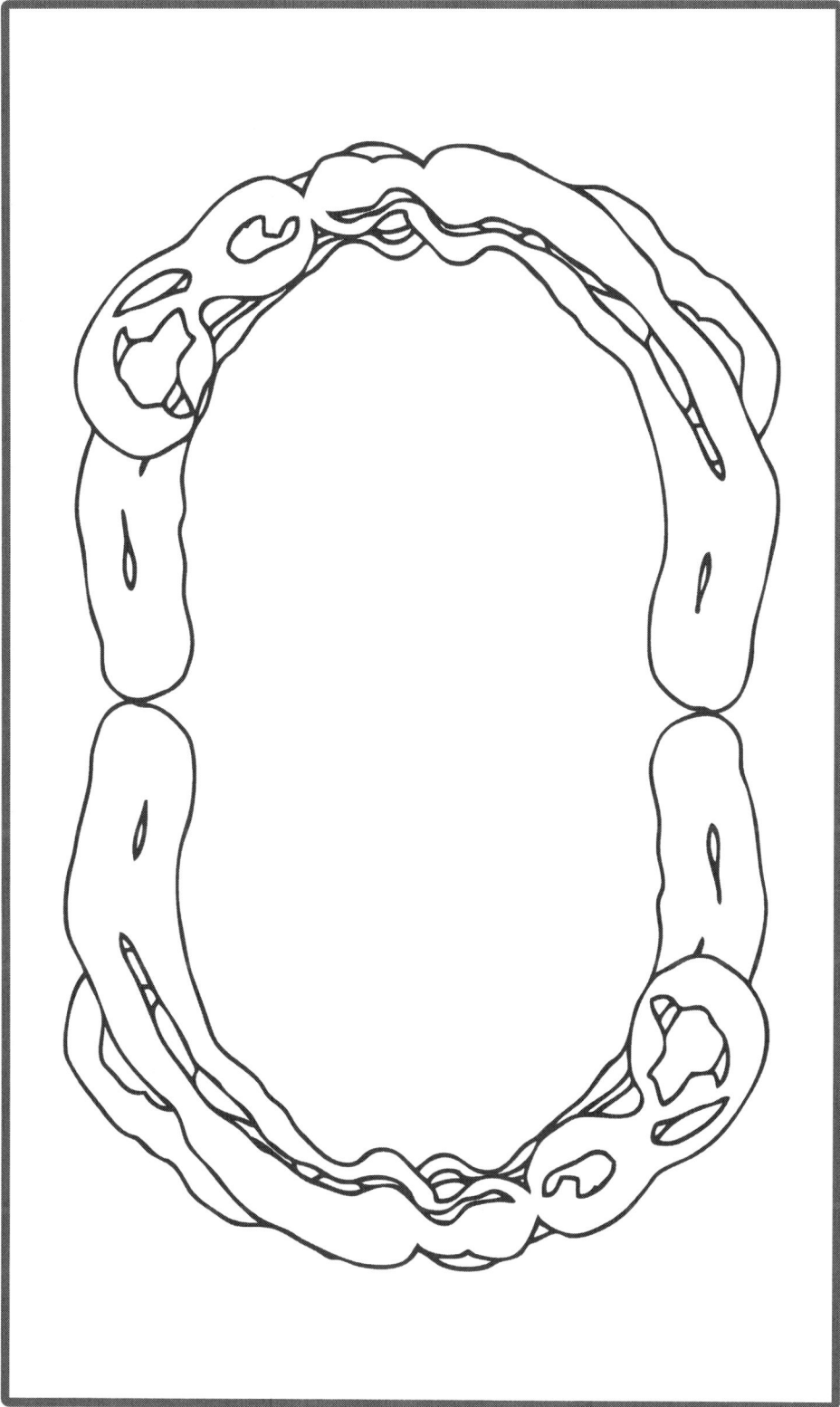

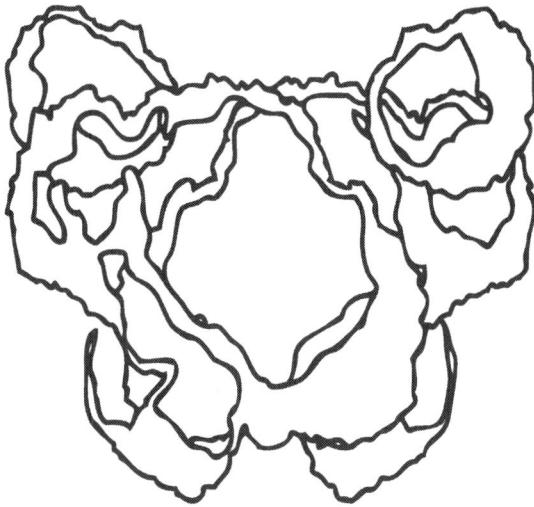

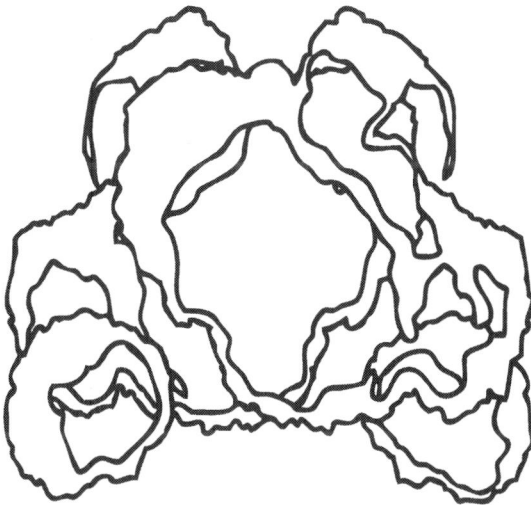

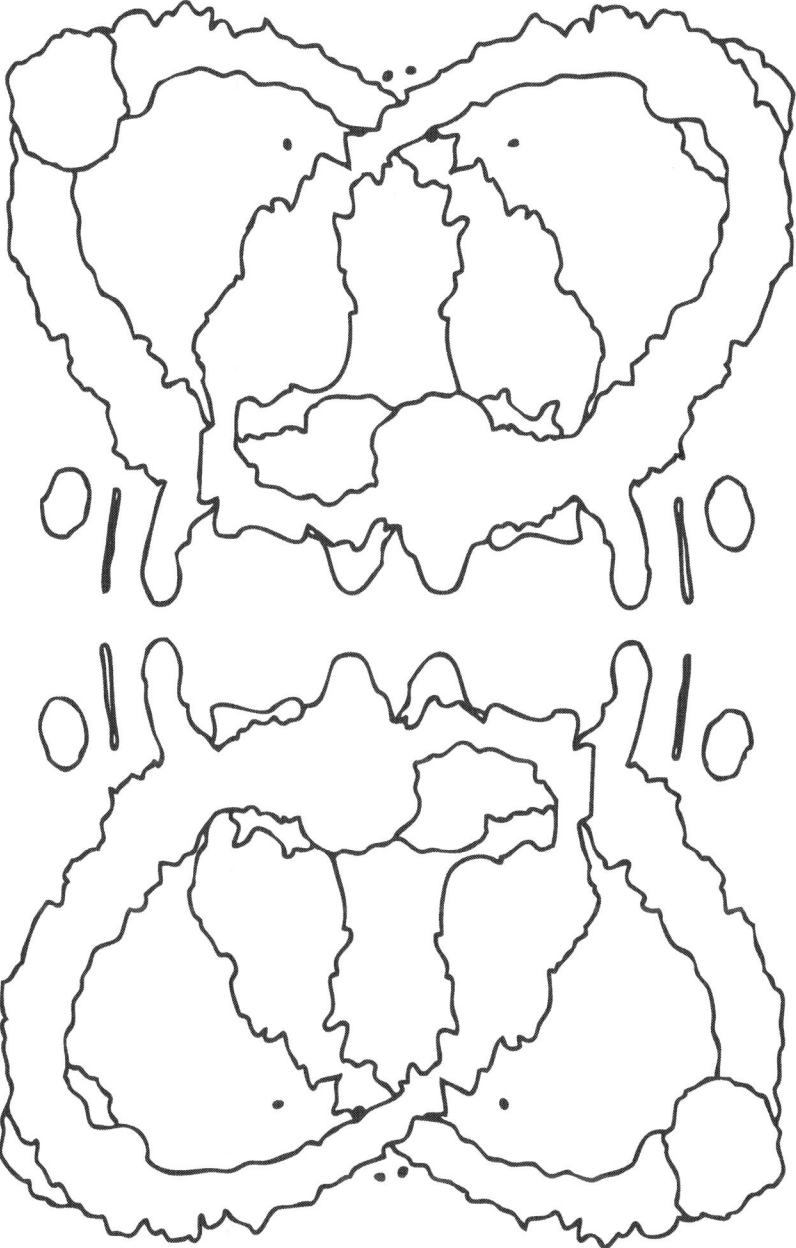

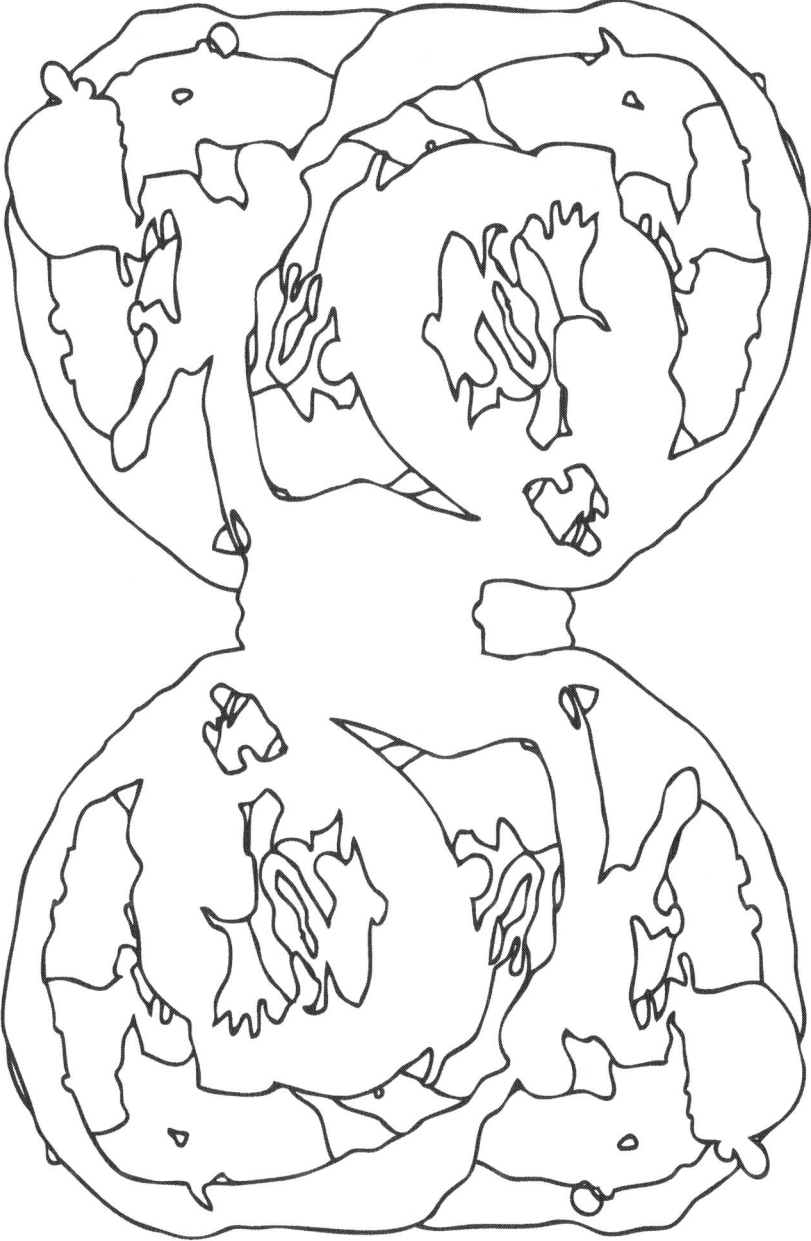

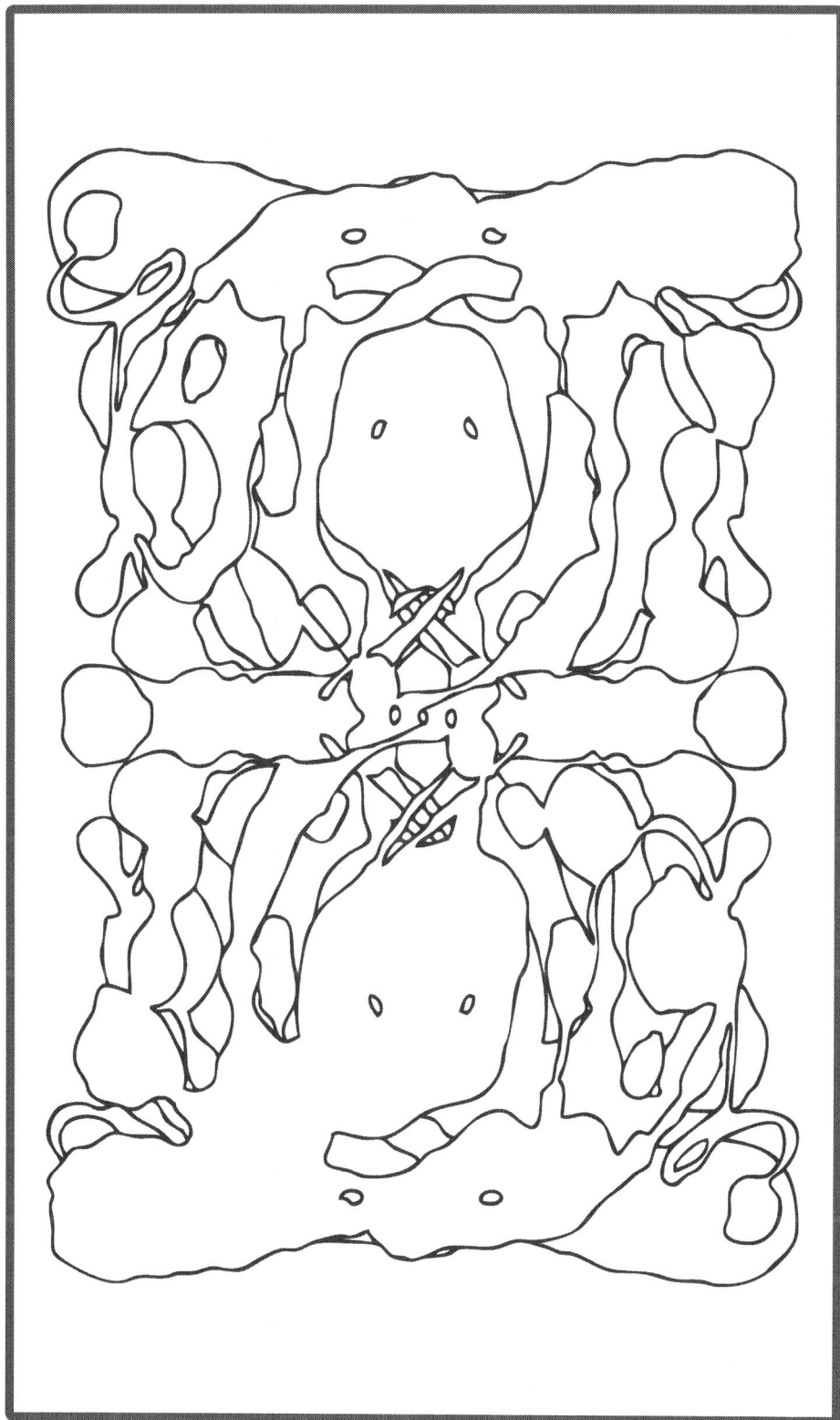

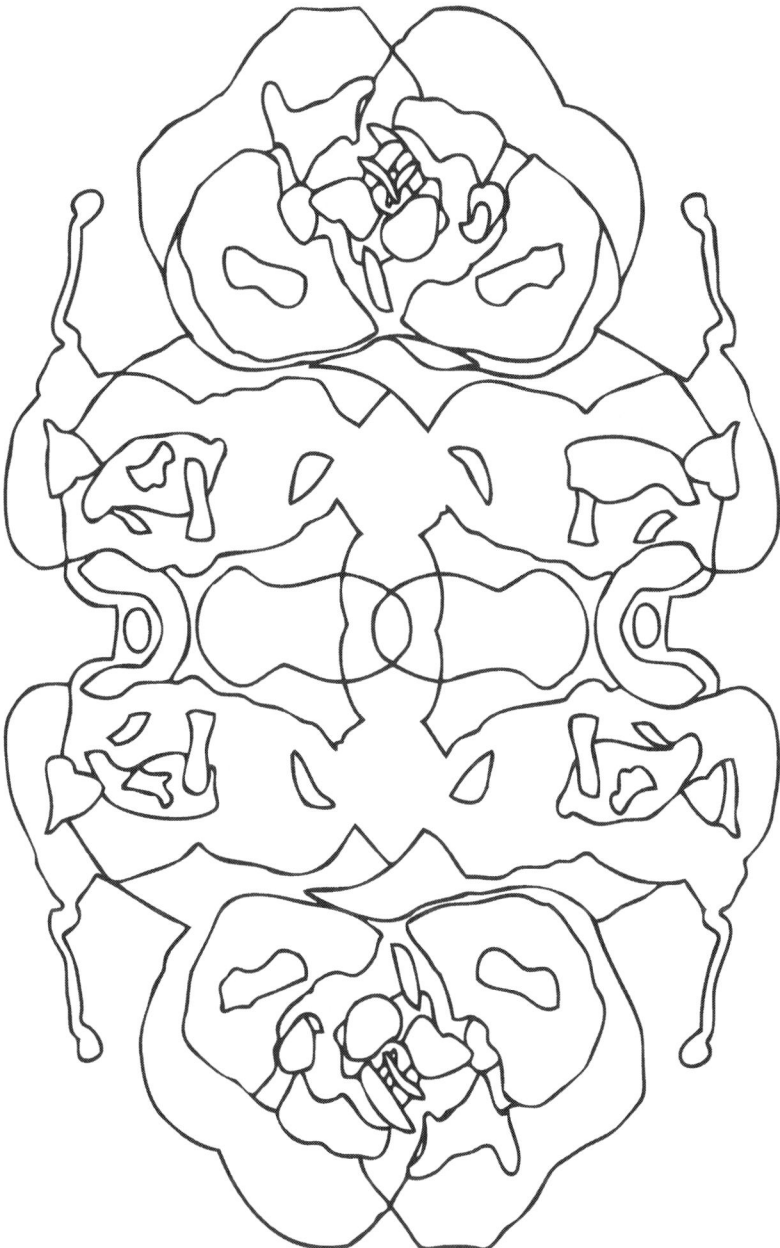

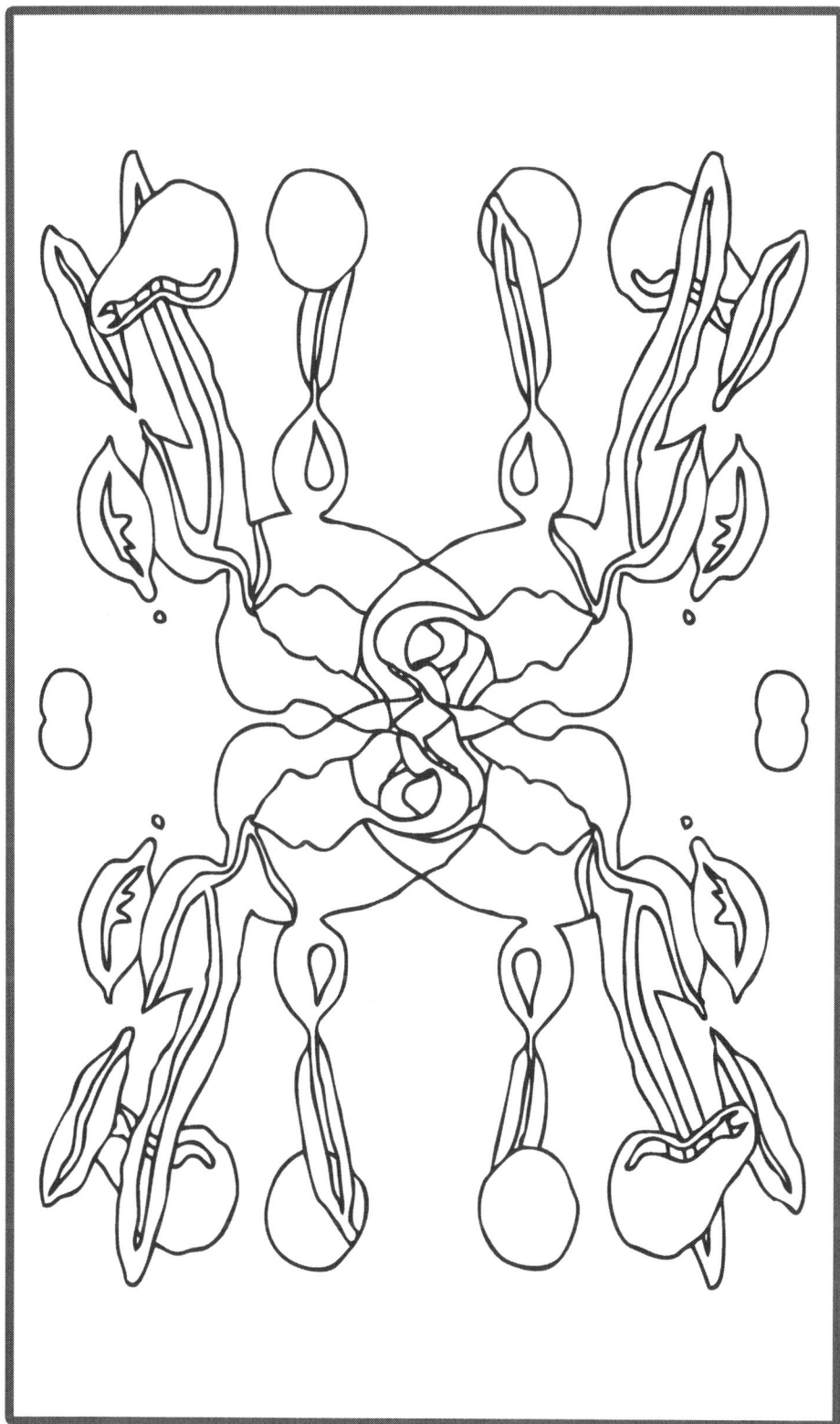

ABOUT ME

Color outside the lines—who cares?

Intrinsically eclectic, silly, and fickle, I'm here to help you have fun! Visit

Keziacarterstudio.com

for free color pages, art tutorials, and original fine art.

Cyberstalk me here:

Made in the USA
Middletown, DE
10 June 2017